THE MORAL CASE ON OUTSOURCING

THE MORAL CASE ON OUTSOURCING

How Good, Bad, or Ugly is it for America and the World?

SCOTT PHILLIPS

ALITUM PRESS
PORTLAND

For information about discounts for bulk purchases,
please contact Alitum Press at sales@alitumpress.com.

First Edition.

Designed by Anita Jones (Another Jones Graphics) and
Olga Bosak (All Elements Design).

Library of Congress Cataloging-in-Publication Data has been applied for.
Library of Congress Control Number: 2011916956

ISBN: 978-0-9846521-3-6 (paperback)

Alitum Press
Box 33
6663 S.W. Beaverton Hillsdale Hwy.
Portland, OR 97225-1403
USA
www.alitumpress.com

1 2 3 4 5 6 7 8 9 0

For my family, whose patience and support have been incredible.

CONTENTS

INTRODUCTION

Introduction

"You're a bad man."

My accuser gave me a disapproving stare and then turned his back and walked away.

As conversations go, it had started on more promising terms. I was traveling to India, and I needed an adapter for my laptop. Standing in the aisle at my local hardware store, I couldn't find the right one.

I asked for help.

The clerk was a slight man in his late forties.

"Where did you say you are going? India?" he asked as we surveyed the row of adapters together.

"Yes, that's right. For ten days. I need an adapter, but I don't see the one I need. Do you think they're sold out?"

"Could be," he said noncommittally, then casually, "Is this a business trip or vacation?"

"It's for work."

He crossed his arms and gave me a sidelong glance. "There sure are a lot of companies taking jobs over there. Is that what you do?"

It was. I hedged. "Er. Sort of. I manage a team of people doing IT support. Some are in India and some are in Canada. I'm going over to meet with the ones in India."

He fixed me with a disapproving stare. "I used to work at [a large local bank]. I was there for fifteen years. I worked in accounting. I lost my job because of people like you." Then he delivered his coup de grace—"You're a bad man"—turned his back, and walked away.

I was left to ponder an encounter with someone who had come out on the losing end of globalization and one of its more controversial manifestations—offshore outsourcing. I never got my accuser's name, but that brief encounter launched the journey that became this book.

At some point, most everyone in the outsourcing industry has had a 'you're a bad man' moment. Perhaps it's at a dinner party where the person across from you mentions someone she knows who has lost their job because of outsourcing. Perhaps it's at a happy hour where you meet a software engineer afraid of losing his.

Outsourcing is a politically charged issue and a social lightning rod. It's a term many Americans have come to associate with everything that is going wrong in America—social contracts broken and good American jobs being shipped over *there,* wherever there is.

As I found myself mentally debating the pros and cons in the aftermath of my encounter, I realized that I had no easy answer to an obvious question: is outsourcing really good or bad for America and the world?

Virtually everyone acknowledges that there is an ugly side to outsourcing when Americans lose jobs. For most, that's where it ends. There is no moral dilemma per se. Outsourcing is simply bad.

But there is a positive side to outsourcing too, and I saw it on my first business trip to India.

I had been to India before. In the mid-nineties I spent thirty days on a backpacking trip around the country, and I came away shocked by the vast scale of poverty, from the slums of Mumbai to the rural farming villages. My reaction was not that of a neophyte traveler in a developing country, though. I had been a Peace Corps volunteer and done a tour in West Africa. I had lived in a rural village, used local transport, and eaten a local diet. I was sure I had seen it all. I hadn't. India stunned me.

That was then.

My next visit came ten years later, and it was immediately clear that big changes were afoot. There was still poverty, to be sure. But there was also a huge boom creating jobs and spreading opportunities far beyond the call center and IT workers in their shiny glass office towers. Driving around Bangalore, I could see these new office blocks springing up all over. They sported the names of the global high technology brands from Dell to HP, Intel to IBM, Oracle to Cisco. They also included the new rising stars of Infosys, Tata, Wipro, and more.

Everyone talks about that skyline—and it is impressive to be sure—but the real story was at street level. That's where I could see that the shops and restaurants were packed, that housing and apartment construction was booming at almost every turn. The place was humming with activity, and it was embodied by the traffic jams. This was emphatic evidence that a lot of people had cars, auto-rickshaws, and motorcycles. I was astonished. Jobs were being created in Bangalore at every level of society in a way that I could only have dreamed of during my Peace Corps volunteer days in Sierra Leone, West Africa.

Something good was happening in India, and this resonated for me. Helping the poor in developing countries was the reason I had volunteered to join the Peace Corps. While outsourcing wasn't directly employing the poor, indirectly there appeared to be a multiplier effect, and outsourcing had something to do with it.

How then, I asked, do we balance this positive against the job loss in America? Are we in a win-lose game, where Americans are always on the losing side? These questions nagged at me, and I frankly had doubts about where the truth might lie. This was a genuine moral dilemma, and I personally wanted to know what the truth really was. I also felt I owed an honest answer to everyone who questions the basis of this industry and the premise of sending jobs to other countries.

That was enough to start the research. But was there really a need for a book about outsourcing, one that wanted to confront the costs and benefits from a political, social, and moral perspective? Ultimately you will judge, but here are four reasons I identified that suggest the answer is yes:

First, outsourcing has captured a central part in the conventional wisdom of most Americans—and not in a good way. Here are some numbers to consider: In the spring of 2006, *Foreign Affairs*, one of America's most prestigious foreign policy journals, reported 87 percent of those surveyed were concerned about outsourcing, and a majority—52 percent—admitted that they worried *a lot* about it.[1]

A survey by the German Marshall Fund of the United States at the close of 2007 found that 61 percent of Americans see outsourcing as the top reason for job loss in the US economy.[2] In the fall of 2008, in the midst of a presidential election cycle, the Pew Research Center reported that nearly 82 percent of Americans believe protecting American jobs should be a top priority of US foreign policy.[3] By the fall of 2010, public support for free trade agreements had fallen to a thirteen-year low with 44 percent of Americans saying they were bad for the United States and 55 percent believing they led to job losses at home. Free trade is only a loose proxy for outsourcing. Public hostility to outsourcing is likely to be hitting new highs as well.[4]

Outsourcing upsets most Americans. They don't like it. They blame it for a lot of the problems facing workers in today's economy. The level of concern has also been remarkably consistent over the last decade and the entire political spectrum.

The second reason the issue of outsourcing is important—now more than ever—is timing. As of this writing, we are still in the aftershocks of the greatest economic crisis since the Great Depression and the first fully global recession since the end of World War II. It is not over yet. The recovery has been anemic and could falter now as it did in the 1930s.

Up until 2008, the economy overall was performing well and the unemployment rate of 4.4 percent (at the end of 2007) was at one of the lowest ebbs in post–World War II history. Yet this low-water mark for unemployment is also the period in which outsourcing was capturing such negative press. Unemployment in early 2012 is still stuck above 8 percent, but including broader measures such as underemployment brings that rate as high as 16 to 17 percent.

In good times and bad, outsourcing is one industry that can expect hostility. The threat of protectionism is very real. At the height of the crisis, the US Congress added 'Buy America' to its stimulus bill. A French president called for the repatriation of French manufacturing jobs from Eastern Europe. The Indian government slapped tariffs on imported Chinese toys. America and China flexed their protectionist muscles over tires and chickens.

That makes this topic urgent, for any future debate about trade and protectionism will almost certainly confront the topic of outsourcing, which lies at the very heart of global supply chains and chronic trade deficits.

The third rationale for this book is that there is a vast gap in the debate about outsourcing. Much of what is communicated is polarized and one-sided. I have yet to find a fair, balanced discussion that clearly lays out the pros and cons across each of the dimensions—political, economic, and, yes, moral.

The opposition only sees the bad. In his book *War on the Middle Class*, Lou Dobbs practically links the downfall of the entire American middle class to companies determined to outsource their jobs overseas.[5]

A simple summary of what opponents think about outsourcing would probably go something like this: Outsourcing is driven by profit and greed and a desire to exploit workers in poor countries, paying pennies on the dollar compared to what Americans would make at home. In the process, the rich get richer (CEOs, wealthy stockholders), while loyal employees at home in America get sold down the river, discarded without due consideration, and left to fend for themselves in an increasingly difficult American economy composed of a few *haves* and a lot more *have-nots*. American workers who once had decent, well-paying careers find themselves on a steep, slippery slope heading for low-income jobs, scratching out a living as part-time workers at Walmart. Meanwhile, those exploited workers in developing countries toil away in dangerous, hazardous factories that spew unregulated pollution into the local environment and the global commons.

This indictment is echoed in the postings you see in blogs and comments on the internet. A few years ago, *Business Week* ran an article with the catchy title, "The Future of Outsourcing."[6] Years later, the article is till attracting controversy and online comments, mostly negative.

On the other side of the debate, proponents commonly cite the business benefits of outsourcing. Their storyline goes like this: Businesses gain competitive advantage by accessing global markets for talent. They get cost savings, but this is only one dimension of the benefits of going global. Even more so, by outsourcing simple, repetitive tasks that can be done cheaply in remote locations, businesses can concentrate on the more high-skill work at home. This focus on high-value jobs at home helps increase the wages for employees in the United States. The cost savings allows companies to reallocate the money for investments and innovations that they could not have afforded otherwise. In the process, companies get stronger, create new products, continue to grow and become more competitive and, thus, generate more jobs in the United States. That, in a nutshell, is the business case for outsourcing. Proponents would say it is a win-win.

These arguments, both positive and negative, make a simple point: the debate tends to be emotional, incomplete, and one-sided. There is clearly a moral dimension. Even practitioners and proponents of outsourcing overtly acknowledge the moral nature of this debate. I once listened to a business journalist giving a lunch-time keynote to an outsourcing conference. He started his address with a moral analogy by comparing America's *perception* of outsourcing as being roughly equivalent to America's *perception* of pornography.[7] (A few salad forks got dropped.) (Caveat. He was not trying to say they were equivalent, merely the perception of them. Still..)

Both sides have good points, and there is truth to both perspectives, yet the subject is largely treated like a legal brief. You are either for or against. It's black, or it's white. While I understand that controversy sells, I wanted to have an adult conversation. I hungered for a book that would lay out the pros and cons and deal with all of the shades of grey that are part of this issue. I didn't find one so I decided to write it.

The fourth rationale for this book is in the realm of political economic strategy. It is the importance of what I call the Or Assumption, and it goes something like this: Do we want America to be a country that outsources all its jobs or a country that does more of x? The x can be just about anything these days—it just depends on who is making the point, an author or a politician, a pundit or a journalist.

In his book *Hot, Flat, and Crowded*, Thomas Friedman uses the Or Assumption to pose exactly this type of rhetorical question. His x stands for green jobs.[8] Mind you, I am a fan of Friedman; this is not a criticism. The point is that it hardly matters anymore what follows the first half of the *or*—or even who is saying it. It has become a rhetorical device for politicians and pundits across the land whenever they are trying to explain the landscape today and their vision of America's future and the challenges it must face up to. Outsourcing has become a metaphor for our fears, a scapegoat for our frustrations and failures. It has become the political-economic equivalent of the boogeyman.

But assumptions can be dangerous—and wrong. Today, it is widely accepted that outsourcing is damaging the American economy and our future prospects. What if that's not true? What if America can be a country that outsources labor-intensive jobs to China *and* a country that creates new industries with high-paying jobs for our own long-term benefit? This is not merely a debate about the risks of sliding into protectionism, but also a fundamental question about how economies transform over time and how we promote growth and prosperity at home as well as abroad. These questions are enormous and—depending on how we answer them—they define how we will relate to the world over the next generation and how globalization, outsourcing, and trade will affect our economy and society.

There is a last reason why I decided to take this from a hobby project to a published book: It's personal. My personal moral dilemma is a classic fall from grace. In this case a sudden descent from wearing a halo to sporting horns and a tail.

The halo came first. Right out of college, I joined the Peace Corps, a US government agency that sends American volunteers overseas for two-year assignments to work in developing countries helping local people. My Peace Corps tour was in Sierra Leone, an impoverished (and beautiful) country on the west coast of Africa. For two years, I lived in the quintessential thatch-roof hut in a remote village in the northeast highlands of the country while I worked with local farmers to improve agriculture practices. After a two-year stint in the field, I returned to the United States and went to work at Peace Corps Headquarters in Washington, D.C., spending another five years in roles that included country desk officer for Nepal, Sri Lanka, and the Philippines.

When the subject of my Peace Corps experience comes up socially, the halo goes on. People nod and concede, "Yes, I thought about doing that, too." But they didn't. The moral high ground can be quite comfortable.

My second career was in information technology (IT). My employer was one of the world's premier IT consulting and outsourcing firms. For six years, the job entailed consulting assignments for various clients on a variety of system integration projects. This was all decidedly neutral in moral terms. It wasn't romantic, but it paid the bills, and engineering a billing system or an e-commerce website didn't cause any harm.

One day the current job was finishing, and I started networking internally for the next project. It was not long before I heard from an old colleague. "Join us over here," he said. "You'll manage an international team for a great client. You'll get to do some international travel."

It sounded great. I signed up.

As quick as that, I transitioned from consulting to outsourcing. Not that I was naïve—I understood the larger social qualms about the industry and even felt them myself. My encounter with the hardware clerk—coming in the early days of my first assignment in outsourcing—made the moral questions immediate, and I started a quest to find the truth. It is one that has lasted several years, far longer than I initially expected.

While the moral high ground may be comfortable, it's the sudden loss of it—socially, emotionally—that focuses the mind. I also felt responsible. I owed that man an answer.

While the first four reasons for writing this book relate to the outside world—the overwhelming concern by most Americans about outsourcing; a global economic crisis that raises the stakes; the gap in the debate in which both sides stake out purely one-sided points of view and neglect to include a balanced accounting of pros and cons; and the Or Assumption that America has to choose either outsourcing or some other destiny to prosper—the fifth reason is purely personal, a quest to explore a moral dilemma and to do the right thing—to explain the impact of this industry both for myself and for others.

Four out of five of these reasons suggest that an attempt to answer the question—Is outsourcing good or bad for America and the world?—contributes something constructive to the debate. The fifth reason is why I had to do it anyway.

To do justice to the questions above, what's needed is a framework for looking at the overall costs and benefits and weighing the impact to both America and the world not just from a political or economic perspective but also from a moral point of view. That framework will help us to determine what the net position really is: good, bad, or ugly.

To provide that framework, this book is organized into four sections: Costs, Benefits, The Moral Case, and Remedies.

Costs

The costs associated with outsourcing get a lot of press, but even the critics miss a few. This section catalogs them—from job loss to wage stagnation, middle-class anxiety to environmental damage, worker exploitation to changing geopolitics. Some indirect effects that aren't often considered, such as the role of outsourcing in the rise of sovereign wealth funds, which have been viewed with alarm by many, are included as well.

Each chapter in this section seeks to determine how outsourcing fits into the larger economic or political puzzle and to quantify, wherever possible, the impact from outsourcing specifically. By cataloguing and analyzing the toll of costs that outsourcing inflicts on America and understanding how this fits into the larger picture of America's political economics, a broad view of the negative consequences of outsourcing can be captured. This list of costs, or consequences, represents one side of the balance sheet, or framework, for the subsequent moral analysis to be done.

Benefits

There are also benefits to offshore outsourcing, and they include—but go beyond—purely increasing business profits or fattening CEO paychecks. My focus is less on the business case to a company and more on the social and economic impacts.

The Benefits section includes a set of chapters that identifies how and where America and American workers benefit, directly and indirectly, from outsourcing. For example, as consumers, we get cheaper goods and services from firms that use outsourcing. The resulting savings benefit people at all income levels, but tend to do so disproportionately at the lower income ranges. We'll explore this scenario and others like it, and where possible, each scenario will be quantified in this section on benefits.

The Moral Case

Having cataloged the costs and benefits in the first two parts of this book, it will then be possible to begin answering the question of whether or not outsourcing is good or bad for America and the world. In The Moral Case section, the reader is introduced to a set of ethical decision models for looking at business and social issues. The models are relatively standard. One example is the Utilitarian model. This is the idea that a decision should be made that does the most good and the least harm for everyone. Another example is the Rights approach, which measures a decision by how well the rights and dignity of everyone involved are respected. These ethical decision models—and more—are accessible to all and provide an independent framework for anyone to do their own analysis.

I then use the Utilitarian model and the data gathered in the first two parts of the book to weigh up the costs and benefits. You deserve an opinion. You'll get it in this chapter. When I first started this book, I wasn't sure where I would land. I am now. I will show you how I weigh up the pros and cons. Then I'll give you my bottom line. You can decide for yourself if you agree or not.

Another chapter in this section will explain how even a perfectly objective framework and analysis won't work with an emotional issue like outsourcing, for the truth is, people are not hardwired for objectivity. Most react at a gut, instinctive level. We'll discuss why this is so and what it means.

Finally, this section explains how the costs and benefits may shift and change over time and how the broader context of America's political economy might shape assumptions about how people approach a moral discussion on outsourcing.

Remedies

The first decade of the new millennium has been a disaster in many respects. The second does not yet look much rosier. We've narrowly avoided a Great Depression, but it has come at a fearful cost. The future looks uncertain. Europe is under pressure and appears to be collapsing along the periphery from Greece to Ireland. Looming fiscal and demographic challenges at home suggest we are in for hard times ourselves.

Regardless of which side anyone comes down on in terms of the moral case on outsourcing, we should all be able to agree that it is important, even urgent, to find a path to prosperity for Americans at all levels of society, especially now, against a backdrop of economic crisis and mass unemployment.

The section on remedies provides an aggressive set of policy recommendations that focus on how to help workers manage the inevitable job and career transitions – whether caused by outsourcing or not, how to help America and all of its citizens prosper in a changing world, and how to cope as a nation that is not just competitive but also prosperous in the face of rising powers like China and India.

These are the biggest of my big ideas on how to help Americans succeed in the face of the vast changes underway in the global economy. They are aggressive. They are specific. You can decide whether they are right.

Caveats and Considerations

The four sections above provide a framework for how to answer the question of outsourcing's impact on America and the world, but there are some additional caveats that should be considered before embarking on the journey.

First, I will explain what is meant by outsourcing and how that is related to globalization. Next, there is the important question of how I can remain unbiased given my guilt by association as a participant in the outsourcing industry. This is followed by a brief discussion of economics and the numbers cited through this book, including the math involved. These fundamental questions set the tone for this book and are discussed below.

What Is Outsourcing?

Outsourcing has become a loaded term in the political lexicon, but it means different things to different people. For some it is a proxy for globalization in general. For others only the jobs going offshore to someplace other than America really matter. At its broadest, some people believe it is any job that could be done in America but isn't. For the purpose of this book, these are the definitions I follow:

Globalization is the trading of goods, services, and ideas across national borders. Getting a cup of coffee today is an example of globalization in action. The coffee you drink may come from Indonesia or Ethiopia. Farmers in one country sell their coffee beans; consumers in another drink the coffee. This is trade between countries, and international trade is not new. It's been going on for millennia. What is new is the speed and breadth of this type of trade. An example is your iPod (or iPhone or iPad), designed in America (by Apple), manufactured in China (by Taiwanese-owned subcontractors), and sold throughout the world to consumers as far apart as Rome and Seattle. Globalization today has a speed and breadth that is much greater than the clipper ships that once plied the China route trading tea for silk.

Globalization is also the spread of ideas across national boundaries and around the globe. It's manifested in movies from Hollywood, downloads from YouTube, and the internet rantings of al-Qaeda. Our world is increasingly interconnected and globalized.

Outsourcing is not the same thing as globalization. When a company hires a vendor to do something that it used to do internally with its own employees, that is outsourcing. This seems obvious now, but outsourcing is a relatively new phenomenon. Peter Drucker is credited as being one of the first to recognize the nascent trend in an article in the *Wall Street Journal* in 1989 called "Sell the Mailroom."[9] Up until that point, most companies were vertically integrated, meaning every job and service was often provided by a company using its own employees. This was long before the idea of core competencies gained currency.

Today, just two decades later, the business world has changed enormously. Companies routinely hire vendors to provide services they once did themselves. Depending on the job, the provider, and what the client wants, this may be done locally by local contractors or overseas by an offshore provider.

Outsourcing is a broad term. It can cover anything and everything from IT work to vehicle maintenance and from accounting to food service. It can result in jobs being sent to North Dakota or Texas, Brazil or India—or staying in the same building and community. If a college campus provides cafeteria food using a vendor rather than its own campus staff, it is outsourcing. The food may or may not be any better, but it does illustrate the point.

Most people aren't worried about outsourcing in general—although there are issues and concerns with its domestic variant. What they are really worried about is jobs going offshore. And that leads us to offshoring.

Offshoring means something quite specific. This is when jobs are moved from one country to another. Offshoring isn't always the same as outsourcing. If a bank hires a vendor and uses the vendor's employees in India rather than its own in the United States, then this is clearly an example of offshore outsourcing. However, if the same bank opens a branch office in India and hires its own Indian employees to work there (often referred to as a captive center), and they do work that used to be done in the United States and is in support of US business operations, then this work has been offshored, but it has not been outsourced.

Here's yet another twist: When a company hires its own employees in a foreign country to support entirely local operations and business in that country (not the United States), then that is neither offshoring nor outsourcing. The jobs were never in the States to begin with.

The differences between outsourcing and offshoring are significant within the industry, but to most people in the public, this is splitting hairs and they don't really care about the nuances. What people are worried about are American jobs going overseas, and that is what this book focuses on. While it's not quite technically correct in this case, *outsourcing* is the term that most people are familiar with. For the purposes of this book, I use both the terms *outsourcing* and *offshoring* interchangeably to mean the jobs going offshore either directly managed by a business itself (offshoring via captive centers) or outsourced to a third-party provider (offshore outsourcing).

Confirmation Bias

Confirmation bias is a term for the unintentional biases built into how a study is constructed and how this bias can impact conclusions. Unwittingly (or not) scientists often exclude data or construct their studies in a way that leads to the conclusion they *wanted* to find, in other words that reinforces a preconceived notion or theory.

If this can be true for a scientist studying something as esoteric as the flight path of a butterfly, it's probably even more so for someone in outsourcing trying to provide a moral framework for the industry (and rationalize his job). Can I really be trusted if I'm in the industry? Having fallen from moral grace and lost my halo, how can I not be biased and want to provide a rationalization that leads me to the conclusions I want to hear? After all, nobody wants to be the bad guy. Can confirmation bias be avoided in this case? The honest answer is no. Not completely. But I can work hard to minimize it through transparency and structure.

The structure in this book is intended to meet this challenge by providing readers with a framework for assessing both the costs and the benefits. Each of the elements on either side of the ledger is discussed, analyzed, and documented. This is open and transparent. Readers are free to do their own homework and thinking on each of the sections independently. New data is always coming available. New headlines splash across the front page every day. The structure in this book allows people to revisit each cost and benefit and decide whether they agree or disagree at each step of the way. The tools—the ethical decision models—are also standard tools available to anyone and are described and referenced so that readers can access them independently. The tools allow readers to add up the elements themselves any way they want.

Thus, this book's structure seeks to overcome the risk of Confirmation Bias by creating a framework that allows readers to weigh the facts themselves, do their own moral analysis, update the balance sheet as new facts come available, and reach their own conclusions, which may change over time.

Economics: The Dismal Science

Even though this is overtly a moral analysis, many elements of the costs and benefits sections rely on economics—which has been called the "dismal science" since the nineteenth century. Other elements of these sections refer to politics, which is even more dismal these days, though slightly less so than finance and banking.

To the best of my ability, I attempt to analyze the findings as they are currently known and reported on. However, economics, more than most sciences, is a body of work subject to great debate and continual interpretation, argument, and reinterpretation. What looks obvious today may be considered totally wrong tomorrow. The only certainty is that it will still be argued in years to come.

Every number cited will be subject to debate, revision, and readjustment. The numbers will change over time. Inevitably, someone will find that I have reported some details incorrectly. Some data will be obsolete before the book is even published. Economists will weigh in with all manner of opinion for and against, much as the causes and responses to the Great Depression are debated by some even today. And that is fine. Debate is healthy. This book is meant to provide a framework of costs and benefits precisely so they can be debated. The value in this book is not in being perfectly right in every element of the framework—or even by having a perfectly all-inclusive framework. The value is in getting people to use a framework in the first place, thereby continually assessing and weighing the moral balance as new information comes available.

Website

I never envisioned this book as a one-way dialogue from me, the writer, to you, the reader. It is with this in mind that I have created a companion website for this book. I encourage readers to offer up their own insights, opinions, interpretations, and comments at *www.themoralcase.com.* The site's structure follows that of this book.

Solid insights and contributions will be identified and highlighted. My intent is to capture the most insightful comments—both for and against—on each area of the book and to use them to upgrade the book and the discussion for everyone.

Leave a smart, insightful comment on either side of the debate, and I may ask you if I can include your quote in the next version of this book.

Conclusion

This book is neither an apology for nor a promotion of outsourcing. It's neither hatchet job nor mea culpa. Instead, it is meant to be an honest attempt to pose—and answer—some very big questions that matter to most Americans.

The first of these are very specific to outsourcing (or offshoring):

- Is outsourcing good or bad for America?
- Is it good or bad for the world?

This book seeks to answer these questions in a balanced, fair way that provides readers with the information they need to develop their own judgment.

I believe a large audience would like to understand what is going on in our economy, how outsourcing fits in, and what the full range of costs and benefits really are. It is for this group that this book is intended.

But the questions posed in this book go beyond outsourcing. In effect, outsourcing has become a proxy for even bigger questions about globalization, the role of trade, the nature of America's economy, and our role in a growing, changing world. Some of these questions are huge in scope:

- How can Americans prosper in a world that has hit 7 billion in population and will grow to 10 billion or more within a generation?
- How can Americans prosper in a world of globalization, outsourcing, and rapid technology change?

Outsourcing has become synonymous with some of our biggest fears and insecurities about both the American economy and our role in the global economy. I have begun to see it as a metaphor for our fears and a scapegoat for our frustrations. It is linked to the rise of China, the closing of American factories, and the erosion of equality in America. It is blamed for the breakdown in the social contract between companies and workers as well as the veritable downfall of the great American middle class. These concerns could well be amplified as we struggle with the aftershocks of the Great Recession.

Against this backdrop, protectionist impulses that would have seemed farfetched just a few years ago are now the stuff of front-page headlines. In the fall of 2010 and early 2011, the dialogue shifted to accusations of a new currency war and confrontations on global imbalances. Then came higher visa fees for outsourcing companies that wanted to bring people to work in the United States.

Action against outsourcing would undoubtedly be welcomed with public approval. An opinion poll by the Pew Research Center on the Press and the People in January 2011 found that 53 percent of Americans believed confronting China on trade was very important. Add to that the 32 percent that thought it was somewhat important and the total is 85 percent of Americans that lean toward tough action on trade with China.[10]

America has also acted unilaterally in the past. In 1971, in the midst of a financial crisis driven by war, trade deficits, and inflation, the Nixon Administration imposed a series of shocks to the Bretton Woods system of fixed exchange rates. One of those unilateral moves was a 10 percent surcharge on all imports. The surcharge didn't last long, but neither did the fixed exchange rates among our trading partners. We have acted before. We may do so again.

Yet we should proceed with caution.

If we have learned one thing from the financial crisis, it is that really smart people don't always make the right call or even have all the information they need to make the best decision. Allowing Lehman Brothers to fail in September 2008 looked like a prudent balancing of risks at the time. In hindsight it led to the implosion of our financial system and required trillions of dollars in public financing to restart the economy, a debt we will be paying back for a generation. Perhaps it would have happened anyway. Perhaps not. Given the chance for a do over, some policy makers and economists might take a different approach with the benefit of hindsight.

In the current environment, outsourcing may provoke special ire from the body politic. But is the conventional wisdom right? What if the benefits outweigh the costs? We ought to ask these questions and be sure, at least relatively, of the answers before we rush to act. If we are wrong, the cure may be worse than the disease at a time when we cannot afford a second affliction.

It is my hope that this book will provide better context to the role that outsourcing plays in our economy. I also hope it will promote a vision for how America and Americans can prosper in an ever-changing world economy that is increasingly characterized by such forces as globalization, outsourcing, and rapid technology change.

PART 1

COSTS

OVERVIEW

THERE IS A DARK SIDE to outsourcing, and everyone knows it—even those in the industry. It manifests as jobs lost at home as well as jobs that don't pay like they used to. It's about a workforce demoralized and anxious, in fear of being made redundant.

There is no shortage of writers and pundits who have documented the stresses pervading the American workforce today, and most of them believe that outsourcing is at least partly to blame. Examples range from Lou Dobbs's *War on the Middle Class* to Senator Byron Dorgan's *Take this Job and Ship It,* from Louis Uchitelle's *The Disposable American* to Thom Hartmann's *Screwed,* from Katherine Newman and Victor Tan Chen's *The Missing Class* to Peter Gosselin's *High Wire* and Clyde Prestowitz's *The Betrayal of American Prosperity.* There is no shortage of such titles.

But job loss and wage stagnation aren't the only moral costs of outsourcing. There are other impacts stemming from the rapidly changing nature of global business, and they entail costs to America and the world, if not to jobs specifically. Examples include labor exploitation, environmental damage, and low-quality products. And these are just the obvious ones. Changes in how global business operates using such tools as outsourcing can have impacts that are less direct. They feed back indirectly into America's economy and society. These negative feedbacks include, but are not limited to, unfair competition, the rise of sovereign wealth funds, and fundamental changes in geopolitical relations.

Some of these negative consequences arise as a result of the rapid economic growth in countries such as China and India that have been the largest beneficiaries of offshore outsourcing. China's growth, for instance, has been enormously influenced by outsourcing. More than half of China's exports, and 90 percent of all electronics, are produced in non Chinese-owned factories.[1,2] A huge number of local suppliers are producing under contract for Western firms. Walmart reportedly has thousands of suppliers in China, the majority of its global supplier base. Outsourcing is, by itself, a significant share of Chinese domestic production and, overall, a catalyst for China's growth as a manufacturing superpower.

In the case of India, Nasscom reports that between 1999 and 2009, outsourcing had grown from 1.5 percent of India's gross domestic products (GDP) to 5.2 percent. It had created more than 2 million jobs directly and another 8 million indirectly. It was also credited for directly increasing India's foreign exchange reserves by 36 percent.

Outsourcing is clearly a big source of growth for destination countries such as China and India. It is, therefore, also indirectly responsible for how growth in these countries impacts the rest of the world, whether that is in the environment, energy prices, or geopolitics.

The chapters in this section attempt to capture a broad range of social, economic, and moral costs that can be attributed to outsourcing, including ones that even the pundits have missed. It seeks to do so in a fair and balanced way, neither flinching from the bad news nor hyping it unnecessarily. An honest accounting is crucial to provide a foundation for considering the moral case on outsourcing and, just as importantly, for determining what to do about it.

Let's start with jobs.

CHAPTER 1

Job Loss

WHILE ECONOMISTS AND BUSINESSPEOPLE talk about job loss in aggregate terms, the truth is that there are real people behind each lost job and for them it is an intensely personal and painful experience. Job loss has a moral cost, and its impacts—both economic and personal—can be measured by the men and women who experience it. The Great Recession of 2007 to 2009 put this human toll in even starker terms as more than 8 million Americans lost jobs, sending unemployment surging from 4 percent to 10 percent. As of the winter of 2012, unemployment levels remained stubbornly high.

The obvious damage when someone loses a job is to income and earnings prospects both immediate and long-term. The Council on Foreign Relations has cited studies concluding that the average laid-off employee makes less in his next job. This effect is more pronounced for people the longer they have been with an employer. Displaced workers with eleven to twenty years of tenure end up making 17 percent less in their next job. The impact is even more severe for those who have served an employer for more than twenty years. They average 30 percent less in their next job.[3]

In a survey of people impacted by job loss in the Great Recession, Rutgers University found that more than half, or 55 percent, of those lucky enough to get a new job took a pay cut. Sixteen percent of the rehires took a pay cut of 11 to 30 percent, while another 13 percent of them took a pay cut of more than 30 percent.[4]

In *High Wire*, Gosselin looks at the pre–Great Recession income loss problem from a household perspective and finds that the odds of a family seeing their income drop by half or more in any two-year stretch was 1 in 11. While there are many reasons for major income drops, job loss accounts for over a quarter.[5]

The economic impact of layoffs is clearly enormous, but Uchitelle in *The Disposable American* makes a succinct case that the personal toll on people from job loss is even worse and spans the range from emotional illness to a broken marriage.[6] Here again, Rutgers' study of the unemployed in the Great Recession makes this more tangible. Researchers found a heavy toll of emotional problems ranging from stress to loss of sleep, from social isolation to anger and—in a small, but significant group of 13 percent—substance abuse. Nine percent of those still unemployed had sought professional help for stress or depression, a number that, if extrapolated out to the larger group of unemployed Americans, would represent more than 1.3 million Americans either seeking or in need of treatment.[7]

If the price is high for individuals who lose their job, it is equally so for communities and the economy as a whole. In economic terms, all of those people who are no longer able to earn a salary at the peak of their potential contribute less in taxes and also consume less, thus supporting fewer jobs. Think of it as the multiplier effect in reverse, another curve in the downward spiral and another contributor to our country's serious fiscal problems. For communities reliant on a few large employers, the loss of a manufacturing plant or the closure of a call center can be truly devastating. Losses like this have been seen over and over again through-out America as industries contract and shift in the face of competition and change.

The moral cost to job loss should be abundantly clear, but how big is the impact from outsourcing? Answering that question requires understanding the scope of total job loss in the US economy (the denominator) as well as the specific share from outsourcing (the numerator).

The Denominator: Total Job Loss

Most people are familiar with the monthly job numbers repeated on the nightly news, and we have seen a litany of these in recent years, a con-stant reminder of the hardships so many fellow Americans suffer. But these monthly numbers are the *net* change, meaning jobs added minus jobs lost equals a monthly number, which is positive or negative. As a net number, these figures barely hint at the true scope of job creation and destruction across the breadth of the economy.

The Bureau of Labor Statistics (BLS) collects data that provides a better picture. One BLS survey is called the Business Employment Dynamics (BED), which is where the monthly net numbers come from. BED data shows total jobs gained and total jobs lost and provides an annual summary that is even seasonally adjusted. If you average the data out from the second half of 1992 through the first half of 2008, it shows that—on average—the economy creates 31.5 million jobs each year and loses a little over 30 million jobs each year. In 2007, a relatively modest year for job growth as housing construction slowed, but before the country went into full economic crisis, the US economy created 30.3 million jobs and lost 29.5 million jobs, a net increase of 731 thousand jobs.[8]

Still, while BED data gives one view of job creation and destruction, it doesn't show the full picture. It looks at the employer level and only counts the net gain or loss for each employer. That means if a company adds 500 workers in one department and lays off 500 workers in another, the net change would be zero and would reflect as zero in the BED data. That view understates total job loss since the 500 who lost jobs in one department are unlikely to be the same people who got the jobs in the other.

To get a truer picture of job loss, look at BLS's Job Openings and Labor Turnover Survey (JOLTS). JOLTS data counts all the jobs created and lost across the economy, not just the net gain or loss. It also very helpfully breaks out job loss into three different categories of separations. These are quits (people leaving voluntarily), layoffs and discharges (people laid off or let go involuntarily), and other (generally retirements and internal transfers). Across all three categories, the annual rate of job loss between 2001 and 2008 was 55 to 65 million quits and separations each year in a workforce of roughly 140 million.

The data for layoffs and discharges is most relevant for our purposes. From 2001 through 2008, the annual average number of layoffs and discharges in the US economy was 23.3 million. In 2007, a good baseline year of moderate, but slowing growth, total layoffs and discharges were 22.5 million.[9] That's a big number, and it represents a huge amount of churn and turnover in America's labor force. The Great Recession caused these numbers to jump significantly. In 2009, total layoffs and discharges was 27.8 million.

The recent economic crisis is supposed to be a once-in-a-hundred-year event. To be conservative (a lower number makes outsourcing losses *more* significant than a higher number), I have used the lower 2007 number of 22.5 million as a baseline of total layoffs and discharges (e.g., people who were fired or laid off, not voluntary quits or transfers) for our analysis.

Now that we have the denominator of total job loss due to involuntary layoffs and separations, we can turn to the portion caused by outsourcing.

The Numerator: Job Loss from Outsourcing

According to the German Marshall Fund survey quoted earlier, 61 percent of Americans see outsourcing as one of the biggest causes of job loss. The conventional wisdom is strongly on the side of outsourcing as a big problem for the American economy and worker.

But is the conventional wisdom right?

The answer to this requires differentiating between manufacturing and services, for each has its own unique dynamics.

Manufacturing Offshoring

Between 2001 and 2004, the United States manufacturing sector lost about 3 million jobs from a total workforce of 17.2 million, a precipitous decline that continued even after the recession of 2001 had ended. After this decline these jobs did not come back, and the cause has been widely debated. Some blame outsourcing. Others suggest that productivity and automation were the main factors. Unfortunately, there is no conclusive data on how many jobs were outsourced to other countries during that period.

Beginning in 2004, however, the BLS began tracking the role of job relocations—called movement of work—among the reasons for mass layoffs and they specifically captured in this data whether the work was moving somewhere domestically or out-of-country. (Mass layoffs are defined as impacting more than 50 people for more than a month and are a subset of total job losses.)[10]

Using 2007 as a good representative year when job loss was not too high and job gains were slowing before the brunt of the Great Recession struck with full force, the data shows that slightly less than 1 million jobs were lost in mass layoff incidents.[11] Of this total, 25 percent of total mass layoffs were in the manufacturing sector—or 230,000 jobs in 2007.

Out of all these mass layoffs, the total jobs lost to movement of work was just over 45,000. Most of these were domestic relocations. Less than 12,000 were identified as out-of-country relocations, a good euphemism for outsourcing. This represents barely 2 percent of total separations from mass layoff events, but since virtually all of these were in the manufacturing sector, it suggests that the rate of manufacturing mass layoffs due to outsourcing to other countries was around 5.4 percent.

If you extrapolate the above percentage (5.4) out to all layoffs and discharges in the manufacturing sector in 2007 (1.96 million jobs),[12] then an estimate of the total annual job loss in manufacturing that may be directly related to outsourcing is in the range of 100,000 to 110,000 jobs lost. This same analytical approach holds for 2005 and 2006, 5.8 percent and 5.6 percent respectively, with the interesting caveat that the rate for job loss due to out-of-country relocations appears to be slowing.

These are relatively modest numbers. After the precipitous drop between 2001 and 2003, total manufacturing employment found a new level of around 14.2 million and drifted down only slightly between 2004 and 2007, until beginning to drop again going into 2008 amidst the full-blown global economic crisis.

Curiously, the 2009 data—in the midst of the greatest economic crisis since the Great Depression—suggests that the volume of offshoring was relatively consistent, but that the rate was lower. The data for 2009 showed approximately 60,000 jobs lost due to movement of work, a higher total number than earlier years. Of these, the data shows that 73 percent of the work relocations were domestic.

But there are gaps in the data for 2009. It was not fully available for about half of the mass layoff incidents caused by movement of work. If we want to be very conservative, we can assume the bulk of these were offshore. Then we are looking at roughly 30,000 jobs relocated offshore. There were 890,618 separations in the manufacturing sector in 2009 due to mass layoff events. Therefore the rate of offshore relocations was approximately 3.3 percent, far lower than previous years. Again, if we extrapolate this out to total jobs lost in manufacturing (2.9 million in 2009), then 3.3 percent, or 99,000, are jobs lost due to offshoring specifically.[13]

The job losses in 2009 were occurring at the same time as the total number of jobs in the manufacturing sector were dropping precipitously by more than 2 million jobs from the start of 2008 to the end of 2009. It is worth noting that estimates of Chinese manufacturing job losses during this same period range from 10 million upward. This implies that those jobs lost in 2008 and 2009 were not going to China, but reflected a massive drop in demand caused by the economic crisis. This method of estimating suggests job losses from outsourcing overseas were relatively modest after 2004. They are not the only estimates available, however.

The AFL-CIO and Working America have been tracking jobs lost due to outsourcing as well. In their recent report, "Sending Jobs Overseas: The Cost to America's Economy and Working Families," released in 2010, they cite a study that estimated outsourced manufacturing jobs at closer to 400,000 per year in 2004.[14] The methodology for this estimate, however, relied on media tracking and used a large multiplier as an estimating factor for what wasn't captured in the media, making their final number hard to confirm. This number does serve to set a potential top-end estimate of the range of job losses from outsourcing, though. One assumes the AFL-CIO would find and quote a study with job loss at the high end. There remains, however, a big difference between my estimate of 100,000-110,00 and theirs of 400,000.

All we know for certain is what BLS captures in its movement of work data as going offshore, and that is quite small. It is in the range of 12,000 to 15,000 in normal years (such as 2007) and as high as 30,000 or more in a bad year (2009). Meanwhile, mass layoffs in the manufacturing sector for all reasons is roughly 200,000 to 250,000. What's surprising is that these numbers, even the top-end number quoted by the AFL-CIO and Working America, are still smaller than what conventional wisdom suggests.

It may not be possible to get to definitive number, but I offer two alternative scenarios: A worst case and a best case.

The Worst-Case Scenario

The real number for job loss could be worse than the estimates we have just discussed. One possibility is that companies are replacing existing suppliers in America with cheaper suppliers overseas, and this is not being accounted for under the movement of work data captured by BLS. The local American supplier companies that are impacted would never have a chance to move work offshore; they would simply lose their existing contracts and it would come under one of the headings indicating a drop in demand, an indicator of lost business. This would be captured in the mass layoff statistics from all causes if they are larger firms. It would not, however, show up in media tracking, which is looking for jobs being moved overseas.

There is also the potential that increased competition from firms that do outsource forces increased productivity (via layoffs) among firms that do not. The jobs moved offshore would be captured in the movement of work data, but the jobs lost as a result by competing firms would not.

Finally, there could be an ecosystem effect in which jobs filter away in small numbers more broadly than is recognized after big factory closures as all of the smaller supplier firms that provide support and parts to larger manufacturers begin to dry up for lack of orders. This could be occurring at scale, but because these firms are very small, it would not be accounted for in the mass layoff statistics and therefore movement of work data. Nor would such job losses in one-, two-, or five-person increments warrant a press release.

All of these factors may result in underestimating the direct and indirect total impact of outsourcing on manufacturing job loss. That would mean the number we have estimated is too small.

The Best-Case Scenario

Total manufacturing employment declined precipitously during 2001 through 2004 and then stayed roughly constant for several years until the Great Recession started in 2007. If job losses due to outsourcing were as high as the critics indicate, then one might reasonably have expected to see a continuing drop-off in total jobs in the manufacturing sector between 2004 and 2007. However, that did not happen.

One possible explanation is that a wave of job loss due to offshoring manufacturing jobs hit hardest prior to 2004 and then subsided, leaving a residual impression of a sector under assault. There are several possible reasons for this, and if there is merit to this contrarian point of view, then it could account for the lower observed numbers in jobs going offshore since 2004 and potentially into the future.

The first reason to consider is that much of what could be offshored had probably already gone by 2004. China, at that point, already produced the vast majority of goods in low-tech, labor-intensive manufacturing like textiles, toys, and consumer electronics assembly. The remaining manufacturing sectors are still under competitive assault, but they are industries in which America has a greater competitive advantage and offshoring is likely to be at a much lower rate. It might still occur, but in smaller numbers and at a slower pace.

Another even more fundamental reason is that the economics of Asia-based supply chains have changed significantly, and offshoring production no longer provides the slam-dunk business case it did in earlier years. China just isn't as attractive as it used to be. *McKinsey Quarterly* first spotlighted this trend in the article "Time to rethink offshoring?" In it, the authors find that the total landed cost of goods made in China and imported to the United States experienced significant cost increases in materials, energy, transportation, and labor by 2008. The cost advantage between onshore production in the United States and offshore production in Asia no longer represented a big cost savings and was potentially negative in some cases.[15] (Note: This is irrespective of other qualitative issues with using overseas suppliers.)

The *McKinsey* authors suggested that managers rethink the economics of offshoring closely and calculate total landed cost not just costs related to labor savings before moving production offshore. (Take a look at the article if you would like a full breakdown of the costs that go into the supply chain. Labor is only one and not the biggest.)

At the same time, findings in the RSM McGladrey 2008 Manufacturing & Wholesale Distribution National Survey, hinted in 2008 that manufacturers might already be doing the math. The survey reported a huge drop in intent to move production offshore—from the low 20 percent range in 2007 (itself a drop from earlier years) to barely 5 percent in 2008. The survey found that the benefits of moving production offshore were shrinking or no longer occurring.[16]

Fundamental changes were clearly happening in 2007 and 2008 with the economics of offshore manufacturing and global supply chains. Then, suddenly, the global economy had a heart attack and went into crisis mode. Prices dropped dramatically for everything from energy to labor. The cost issues underlying global sourcing evaporated as an issue and stayed that way for nearly two and a half years. Until recently, in fact.

At the start of 2011, with the global economy in early recovery, many of the underlying cost trends of higher energy, labor, materials, and transportation costs returned to the forefront of attention, along with speculation that global supply chains might actually start to rebalance with some manufacturing activating starting to come back onshore.

In May 2011, the Boston Consulting Group released its own study called "Made in the USA, Again," which suggested that a renaissance in American manufacturing was at hand. BCG estimates that the total cost advantage (labor, shipping, etc.) of producing in China compared to the United States will drop to single digits or be eliminated entirely by 2015. Labor-intensive products such as textiles and consumer electronics will stay offshore, migrating from China to lower-cost-production locations such as Vietnam or India. But other products that require less labor and are produced in smaller batches, everything from household appliances to construction equipment, are likely to come back and be made in America again.[17]

When several elite consulting groups start saying the same thing, it's time to pay attention. The underlying economics of manufacturing goods in China are changing. If this trend is borne out, we will likely witness a modest revival in manufacturing in the United States with a corresponding increase in total manufacturing employment.

The best case scenario does not imply things have changed completely. In an article in a special report of the Harvard Business Review in March, 2012, Michael E. Porter and Jan W. Rivkin suggest that American managers are still choosing locations outside of the United States in nearly two thirds of business location decisions. Intriguingly, they also point out that these decisions may not be the best choice given the economics of offshore supply chains and hypothesize that managers may only be looking at offshore labor cost instead of the complete picture of the direct and indirect costs of offshoring production. They conclude that, in many cases, there is a strong case for improving manufacturing operations in America rather than moving it overseas.[18]

The best case scenario—if it is true—will take time to prove out over the next few years.

Summary

The bottom line is that there is significant uncertainty about all of the estimates currently available. The direct evidence of offshore job losses captured by BLS is quite small and relates only to mass layoff events. Everything else is an estimate. My own estimate extrapolates the mass layoff numbers out to all manufacturing job losses in a given year using the same estimating factor and yields an estimate in the range of 100,000 to 150,000 jobs lost to outsourcing offshore. This estimate was for a period in which total manufacturing employment was relatively stable at around 14 to 14.4 million. There are, however, estimates that are much higher. To be conservative, I've doubled my estimate for the purposes of this book.

Despite the limitations in both the data and the methodology, it appears that a reasonable estimate of the current rate of direct annual job loss in the manufacturing sector due to offshore outsourcing is in the range of 200,000 to 250,000 jobs lost per year.

Services Offshoring

Outsourcing in the services sector entails activities in the business process outsourcing (BPO) and information technology (IT) sectors. With the service sector accounting for well over two thirds of the US economy, there is understandable concern about our vulnerability to jobs going offshore in this massive sector. It is important, then, to understand how significant this is.

A McKinsey Global Institute study in 2005 estimated job loss from offshoring at "no more than several hundred thousand per year." They based this on their estimate for the demand paired up against the supply of suitably skilled and trained resources.[19]

In 2009, Nasscom, the trade body representing the Indian IT and BPO services market, forecasted a total addition of 226,000 new service jobs (on top of 2.23 million total workers currently employed) to be created in India in fiscal year 2009, down from 375,000 new jobs in fiscal year 2008.[20] About 80 percent of India's BPO and IT headcount is related to export services, such as work performed for clients in the United

States and other countries. Thus, about 180,000 jobs were expected in the outsourcing industry in India in fiscal year 2009, down from about 300,000 created in fiscal year 2008 from outsourcing to India from countries like the United States and the United Kingdom.

A general trend has been that about two thirds of all US offshoring goes to India, and the US market represents about two thirds of offshoring from all sources that is sent to India. That suggests that the total export headcount for India reported by Nasscom is a good estimate for total jobs going offshore from the US services sector. It's an admittedly rough estimate, but directionally should be reasonable. Using this approach to estimate job loss and utilizing the fiscal year 2008 number as a baseline (rather than the smaller fiscal year 2009 number), a reasonable estimate of annual US job loss in the services sector from offshoring is in the range of 250,000 to 300,000 per year.

As an interesting postscript, Nasscom's fiscal year 2010 report showed that total job growth in the Indian IT-BPO sector (overall) in 2009 was actually just 90,000, far lower than the earlier estimate.[21] A year later, Nasscom's fiscal year 2011 report showed a big jump, a net gain of 240,000 jobs across the entire outsourcing industry (domestic and export) as growth rebounded in the face of pent-up demand following the global recession. This latest report indicates that India captured 90 percent of new incremental demand in the global outsourcing market in 2010 and that US demand represented a 61.5 percent share of the Indian export sector. Discount the domestic portion of the net growth in jobs (15 percent to be conservative) and assume US jobs were just 65 percent of the total, and it appears that the net outflow of jobs from the US was in the range of 130,000 to 135,000.

Given the actual results in 2010 and 2011, the estimate of 250,000 to 300,000 jobs lost in the service sector each year in the US seems like a very reasonable range for our study. It is worth, however, considering worst-case and best-case scenarios as additional data points when evaluating services.

Worst-Case Scenario

In his seminal analysis of offshoring in a 2006 article in *Foreign Affairs* magazine, Alan Blinder, a former vice chairman of the Board of Governors of the Federal Reserve, suggests that offshoring would be a "third industrial revolution" that will play out over the next several decades. He believes that the quantitative impact of this revolution may have significant qualitative repercussions as well and that American policy is currently ill-equipped to manage the massive changes that would result.[22] In round numbers, Blinder's rough estimate is that the number of service sector jobs vulnerable to offshoring is in the range of 40 to 42 million, or three times total manufacturing employment.

These are alarming numbers. Even if, as Blinder suggests, it occurs over a period of several decades, it implies a potential run rate of annual job loss as high as 2 million per year annually for two decades. Compared to a run rate that is a tenth of that now, this is worrisome. This is a worst-case scenario and an important top-range estimate to consider.

Best-Case Scenario

My own impression is that the estimates above—including my own—are overly biased to the high side. Why might that be the case? Here are a couple of points to consider:

First, the actual rate of growth in India based on head count has been lower than even my own estimate. The 2010 data is telling, given that it reflected a boost of pent-up demand. Not every year will look like that.

Next, growth in the industry has been substantial, but the pool of new clients is not unlimited. Nasscom itself indicates that it is beginning to look at new industries and markets beyond the United States and the United Kingdom for future growth and that a big share of that will come from other regions and markets. This does not seem to imply a massive increase in the rate of job loss in the US service sector.

In addition, my own experience is that a job gained in India is not necessarily a 1:1 relationship with a job lost in the United States. The savings entailed in offshoring a set of tasks means that a company has been able to afford to put more resources on a task offshore than at home, and companies frequently choose solutions that use a leveraged pyramid with a greater number of more junior resources than is possible at home. This means the numbers of jobs gained in India is higher than the numbers of jobs lost in the United States.

Last, supply constraints of suitable talent are increasingly driving wage inflation that eventually may make utilizing Indian offshore resources less attractive to US companies. There is some anecdotal evidence to suggest this is already occurring. In August 2010, the CEO of Genpact, an Indian call center operator, suggested that the cost advantage between Indian resources and American in some less expensive states had narrowed significantly and that Indian outsourcing companies would be hiring more non-Indians.[23]

Put all of these factors together and I suspect the estimate I have provided of 250,000 to 300,000 jobs lost each year is biased to the high side and may in fact slow significantly as the cost advantage of using Indian resources begins to recede. The best-case scenario, therefore, is for the rate of growth in the industry to slow or remain steady at an average that is closer to 150,000 per year.

Summary: Job Loss

Based on the analysis above, a reasonable, albeit rough, estimate of total annual job loss for both the manufacturing (200,000 to 250,000) and service (250,000 to 300,000) sectors in the United States is in the range of 450,000 to 550,000 jobs per year. Using the 22.5 million base rate for annual layoffs and separations, the rate of job loss from offshoring represents about 2.0 to 2.5 percent of total layoffs and discharges in the US economy each year. If, however, we used either the higher long-term annual job-loss average (23.7 million) or even the 2009 peak (27.8 million), then the share of job loss in the US economy caused by outsourcing offshore would shrink to less than 2 percent of all jobs lost in the American economy.

Despite the relatively small percentage of total job losses across the economy, the total number of jobs lost (450,000 to 550,000) is significant, can be devastating to individuals and communities impacted, and represents a moral and social toll on American workers and the US economy that should be accounted for in our weighing of the moral costs and benefits of outsourcing.

CHAPTER 2

Middle Class Anxiety: Wages & Costs

DURING THE EARLY NINETIES, President Clinton's Secretary of Labor Robert Reich coined the term *anxious class* to describe the pervasive anxiety within America's middle class. Testifying before Congress about the impact of increasing global competition from Europe and Japan from the 1970s onwards, he said:

> A global economy made competition more fierce and jobs less certain. Labor unions, once a middle class staple, declined. And new technologies—especially the personal computer—revolutionized the workplace, and eliminated many routine mass production jobs. As the economy changed, middle class families tried every means of holding on: Spouses went to work, both parents worked longer hours or took multiple jobs, they decided to have fewer kids and have them later, and they drew down their savings. But families have pushed these coping mechanisms about as far as they can go. Our middle class has become an anxious class.[24]

Writers have been capturing a widespread level of anxiety throughout the American workforce and middle class ever since. What specifically is causing this middle class anxiety?

Middle Class Anxiety: The Wage Problem

The first factor in middle class anxiety is stagnant wages. Steven Greenhouse, author of *The Big Squeeze*, wrote in 2008 that median income had fallen by $2,400 to $54,726 since 2000.[25] A study by Jared Bernstein of the Economic Policy Institute also reported that in inflation-adjusted 2007 dollars, household income fell by $324 between 2000 and 2007.[26]

However you cut the numbers, it is clear that wages have fallen for households during the most recent economic cycle that started in 2000, and this was before the Great Recession fully hit at the end of 2008. Many now consider the last ten years a lost decade for American workers in terms of wages.

What portion of this decrease in wages for working Americans is caused by outsourcing? A recent Pew survey found that 45 percent of Americans view free trade, including outsourcing, as a cause of lower wages in the United States.[27] Are they right?

In *The State of Working America, 2008/2009*, the Economic Policy Institute suggests that about one third of the cause of wage inequality is related to a mix of globalization (immigration, trade, and capital mobility) as well as shifts away from manufacturing toward lower-paying services industries.[28] Thus, offshoring is bundled up among a number of factors that are only a part of the cause.

A more comprehensive analysis of the role of global trade in wage stagnation and inequality is from Robert Lawrence at the Peterson Institute for International Economics. In *Blue-Collar Blues*, Lawrence calculates that trade reduced blue-collar wages by 1.4 percent between 1981 and 2006. However, almost all of the effect hit before 2000. In manufacturing, trade has had negligible impact on wages. In services it may have had some impact, although this is not fully clear from the available data.[29]

In another analysis, McKinsey Global Institute finds that 71 percent of American workers are either in jobs that have low demand from employers (resulting in low or stagnant wages) or jobs for which there is an oversupply of workers (again resulting in low or stagnant wages).[30] Some jobs are in lower demand because of a mix of trade, foreign direct investment, and offshoring, but it is not the only factor. Other factors include the role of skill-based technology change, immigration, aging, and de-unionization.

McKinsey's point, however, is that wages are stagnant for a broad swath of American workers because they do not have the skills to move into jobs that are in high demand because those jobs require higher levels of education. The report suggests strongly that upgrading the skills of Americans currently in the workforce is a critical imperative.

Anecdotally, there are media reports of a shortage of skilled manufacturing workers as employers seek qualified employees who can operate complex computerized equipment, calculate reasonably complex math equations, and solve problems. This shortage comes even in the midst of record unemployment and a jobless recovery that has left manufacturing workers redundant and looking for jobs.[31] This lends some credence to the McKinsey analysis above.

The debate over the causes of wage stagnation will continue for some time. However, the evidence seems to indicate that offshore outsourcing is just one element that has impacted wages since 2000 and is a relatively small influence. The other factors that may have had more of an impact include technology-driven productivity gains, failure to increase the minimum wage, displacement of wages due to the rising cost of benefits, increased competition, and a broader lack of education and skills across the American workforce—meaning many workers cannot move into better paying jobs.

Middle Class Anxiety: The Cost Problem

If wages were the only story, the problem might seem manageable, but that is not the case. At the same time that wages have stagnated or decreased for most American families, costs have been increasing for a range of core public services from health care to college education. These cost increases are the other side of the equation that is squeezing the middle class and causing widespread anxiety.

In the case of health care, the Kaiser Family Foundation reports that workers and employers in the United States were projected to spend over $2.5 trillion on health care in 2009, an average of $8,160 for every US resident. Since 1999, health insurance premiums have risen 119 percent while workers' earnings have risen just 34 percent during the same time period. Americans are increasingly anxious about rising costs. The Kaiser Family Foundation reports that 45 percent of Americans are very worried about having to pay more for their health care, and 53 percent say their income is not keeping up with rising prices.[32]

The picture in higher education is equally stark. According to the Measuring Up 2008 report, while family income has risen by 147 percent since the 1980s, college tuition and fees have increased by *439 percent* during the same period.[33] The dramatic rise in higher education costs is leading to more deeply indebted college graduates whose financial prospects are then hurt by the cost of carrying all that debt. More importantly, the increasingly high price may be pushing down the number of people willing to invest in higher education and causing a higher proportion to drop out before finishing. This is occurring even as the global economy shifts more toward knowledge-intensive industries and other countries are working hard to become more educated and competitive.

With all of these increasing hits to the middle-class family budget, what is increasingly at risk is the American Dream. A majority of Americans, 79 percent, say it is more difficult than just five years ago for people in the middle class to maintain their standard of living. While two thirds say their standard of living is better than that of their parents, barely 50 percent believe their children will do better than they have.[34]

The rising cost of public services is an underlying component of American middle class anxiety. But what is also true is that these sectors are the least able to achieve productivity gains. Alan Blinder, an author and former Federal Reserve Board member, suggests why this is so: the "cost disease" of personal services, as identified by economist William Baumol. Productivity improvements are highly undesirable in some industries. For instance, most people don't want teachers teaching larger class sizes, so their productivity is expected to stay the same, not to increase. Neither do most people want doctors seeing multiple patients at the same time or for much shorter times so they can attend to more patients in a day. Because certain types of personal services cannot achieve productivity gains and because real wages are always rising, personal services like education and health care, unlike manufactured goods, grow ever more expensive over time.[35] The irony here, of course, is that these critical services continue to increase in price precisely because they *cannot* be outsourced.

The rising costs of health care, education, and other public services are important culprits in the picture of middle-class anxiety. However, there appears to be no direct causal link to offshore outsourcing.

CHAPTER 3

Labor Exploitation

LABOR WAGE ARBITRAGE is a fundamental part of the business case in any outsourcing decision. But if American jobs are being shipped to places where workers receive just pennies on the dollar, labor under abusive and unsafe conditions, and are severely exploited, then there is clearly a moral cost to the outsourcing of these jobs with an associated moral burden that must be accounted for.

In his book *The Coming China Wars*, Peter Navarro levels a common accusation that Chinese factories are the worst kind of Dickensian sweatshops, and he compares them to the most dangerous American factories exposed by the muckrakers one hundred years ago.[36] To what extent is this view correct? There are two primary sides of outsourcing to consider: services and manufacturing.

The services side of outsourcing—at least among large companies—is characterized by reasonably safe work environments, ever-rising wages, and a management that caters to people's career desires and personal engagement with the workplace. People are free to leave, and they often do as soon as they find an opportunity to advance their career or income. This is true regardless of country—India, China, or the Philippines. I am not aware of any endemic labor conditions that could be considered abusive or exploitative in the services industry, although such conditions may exist in smaller firms or in isolated cases in larger firms. It is not, to the best of my knowledge, the norm.

The picture on the manufacturing side, however, is not so positive. In the case of China (which is likely similar to many other countries), nonprofit organizations such as the China Labor Watch[37] and the China Labour Bulletin[38] routinely catalog accusations of labor abuses ranging from unfair wages and failure to pay overtime to unsafe working conditions and exposure to toxic chemicals. Many such cases have been documented among companies that supply Western firms as varied as Walmart, Adidas, and Foxconn, to name just a few recent examples. This continues to occur despite new labor laws enacted by the Chinese government and after a decade of activism by nonprofits to promote better working conditions. Many Western companies have set up their own inspection systems ostensibly to ensure their suppliers are in compliance with local laws. The results have been limited, however.

Alexandra Harney, in her book *The China Price*, describes a system in which most multinational companies have set up conflicting departments in charge of purchasing on the one hand and compliance with working standards on the other. The purchasing departments ruthlessly push their suppliers for cost cuts as they drop and add suppliers based on price. Meanwhile, the compliance teams—often understaffed and inexperienced—attempt to audit factories to determine if they are meeting labor standards. The two functions are at odds, but the purchasing departments usually make the final determination on which suppliers to use—and this call is mostly based on price, not compliance.[39]

Outsourcing as an industry has helped to create labor abuse in its supplier bases and is directly responsible for much of it. From a moral perspective, labor exploitation by companies outsourcing their production to developing countries—whether directly managed and owned or indirectly purchased through suppliers—is a moral cost to be addressed and accounted for. Dealing with it may require fundamentally changing how business is done with suppliers.

Workers, however, are not completely acquiescent in this picture, as the highly publicized strikes in June 2010 demonstrated. First, a scandal involving worker suicides at Foxconn factories resulted in intense media focus on the difficult working conditions for China's factory workers. Foxconn, forced to review its policies and pay structures, ultimately doubled salaries for all its workers. While conditions are presumably better at Foxconn as a result, a spotlight had been put on the issue of labor exploitation and the grievances of Chinese workers.

In the midst of the Foxconn controversy, more strikes broke out simultaneously at several more factories around southern China. At Honda's factory in southern China, workers walked out demanding higher wages and the right to form their own union. Ultimately, the workers won a double-digit increase and better benefits, although the package was lower than what they had first demanded.

For many, these incidents suggest that costs are set to rise when it comes to Chinese labor. Workers are also growing scarce due to demographic trends within China, granting stronger negotiating leverage and forcing higher wages.

After China introduced tough new labor laws at the start of 2008, labor disputes taken to Chinese courts nearly doubled, reaching 286,000 that year. Chinese workers are now aware of, and more willing to use, the laws to file suit when they believe employers are not treating them fairly or legally.[40] In 2009, labor disputes filed in China's court system increased to over 318,000, and 2010 brought 207,400 disputes filed in just the first eight months.[41]

These are all positive developments and may ultimately lead to better working conditions and pay. However, outsourcing as an industry deserves no credit for these improvements, as they are being driven by workers themselves. The industry's efforts to foster better working conditions too often takes a lower priority to the desire to procure goods at the lowest possible price. The moral cost of labor exploitation remains high and the industry must shoulder its share of the blame.

CHAPTER 4

Environmental Damage

IN 2007, CHINA eclipsed the United States as the world's biggest emitter of carbon dioxide and accounted for two thirds of that year's global increase in greenhouse gas emissions.[42] Projecting to 2030, the International Energy Agency forecasts that more than 50 percent of the increase in global energy demand between now and then will come from China and India.[43]

Chinese officials attribute between 15 and 25 percent of their country's carbon emissions to the production of exports. That adds up to 1 to 2 billion metric tons of carbon dioxide that is entering the atmosphere each year due to outsourcing, and Chinese officials believe it is unfair for them to pay for cutting emission levels caused by the demand of other countries.[44] As this debate rages on, the question remains: what is the moral cost of outsourcing's impact on the environment?

There are really two facets to this. The first is the impact on the global commons—in effect, pollution that impacts everyone. This includes greenhouse gases that affect climate change as well as other pollutants in the air and water that impact people around the world. The other element of moral cost is to the local environment spoiled by smog-filled air, polluted waterways, and toxic chemical dumps. In both cases, outsourcing must account for a significant share of the moral cost.

Had the production that is currently taking place in China remained in advanced countries, it would still have used energy and produced emissions, but that energy might have been cleaner and more efficiently produced. After all, China relies heavily on coal plants that use older, cheaper, and dirtier technology. The true net increase from moving production to China is likely to be between 25 and 50 percent of the total emissions produced by the Chinese export sector—roughly

0.5 to 1 billion tons of carbon dioxide each year (my rough estimate assuming Chinese coal plants are two to three times more polluting than comparable Western ones).

However, there is also the catalytic effect that outsourcing has had on Chinese growth. This includes the rapid build-out of infrastructure from highways to skyscrapers as the Chinese economy industrializes and urbanizes. While this growth would likely have occurred over time, outsourcing has helped accelerate it.

Locally, the cost of pollution is devastating as well, and China's local pollution was recently quantified in human terms. A World Health Organization study estimated that deaths in China from air and water pollution totaled 750,000 per year. The Chinese government disputed the study, and it has not been released by the WHO.[45] Regardless of what the final number is, China—and other countries booming with business due to outsourcing—suffer environmental consequences.

There is clearly a moral consequence to the environment from the rapid economic growth in China, and a significant portion of this is directly caused by Western firms and their production facilities, or those of their subcontractors. The pollution they produce spoils the global commons and the local environment.

CHAPTER 5

Bad, Dangerous Products

ONE MAJOR CONCERN that offshoring critics have long been pointing out is the quality and safety of goods outsourced to low-cost countries and sold in America. When research for this book began, the evidence for this claim seemed scant, and I was initially skeptical. Then headlines started exploding across front pages around the world, mostly involving unsafe products from China.

First there was seafood with traces of chemicals and antibiotics, and then there was pet food laced with poison. Then revelations of lead paint in toys, followed by toxic pajamas, and medicines with fake additives. This last scandal involving Heparin, a blood thinner, was linked to multiple deaths in the United States. The problem was apparently caused by unscrupulous local Chinese suppliers providing tainted or fake raw ingredients to a factory in China owned by Baxter International, a multinational that produces most of the Heparin sold in the United States.

While Chinese government officials have claimed that the vast majority of products from China are safe, the evidence suggests problems are pervasive—and much of the criticism is valid. The European Union, for instance, found in 2007 that the number of dangerous products recalled from stores jumped 53 percent in 2007 (from 1,051 to 1,605 recalls), and 52 percent of these recalls were caused by products made in China.[46]

Not every problem is caused by Chinese suppliers and their manufacturing quality, however. In 2007, Mattel, which produces two thirds of all its toys in China, was forced to recall 21 million toys made in China—including ever-popular Barbie dolls and toy cars—due to concerns about lead paint and small magnets that could be swallowed. Most of the finger pointing was initially aimed at China. Then it emerged that the problem was actually one of poor design by Mattel's own product engineers. Mattel was forced to make an unprecedented apology to the Chinese government.[47]

In fact, one study of recalls in the toy sector found that design problems were the cause of 61 percent of all toy-related recalls since 1988.[48] In at least the toy sector, manufacturing – outsourced or otherwise – is not the only problem.

It is apparent that outsourcing is responsible for many of the unsafe products sold in our stores and that there are several interrelated causes. It starts with designing products that are not safe and extends to problems in manufacturing ranging from supplier fault to the failure to test products before they are shipped to stores for consumers to buy. These problems suggest that multinational companies have frequently failed in their duties to design, source, and test products adequately.

The problem of unsafe products, however, is also shared by governments at both the shipping and receiving ends. Both China and the United States have suffered recent scandals with unsafe products made and consumed in their home markets. China had to recall milk and baby formula products that were tainted with melamine, a chemical additive, which caused several deaths and hundreds of thousands of illnesses in young children across China. In the United States, peanut butter tainted with salmonella had much the same impact, albeit on a smaller scale. Both problems are related to poor inspection and compliance systems by their respective governments, creating pervasive quality issues in both the United States and China.

Whether it is fake medicine or tainted food, there is a moral responsibility and cost when unsafe or even lethal products arrive on store shelves, no matter where those shelves are. Companies—whether they outsource their production overseas or keep it at home—must live up to their responsibilities to ensure the safety of those products. There is a clear moral cost when unsafe food and drugs enter our market and put consumers and children at risk.

The moral cost from outsourcing from the recently publicized scandals—as well as the ones that have not captured the headlines—is clear, and it is measured in the deaths of pets and loved ones and the illnesses of thousands. It should be weighted appropriately in any analysis of the moral costs and benefits of outsourcing.

CHAPTER 6

Commodity Inflation

FROM 2003 TO 2008, the global economy experienced a boom in commodity prices for energy, metals and minerals, and, toward the end of the cycle, agricultural goods. The World Bank reported this boom, or super-cycle as it has been called, as the biggest of its kind in over a century, with prices jumping and the peak holding until the global economy plummeted into recession at the end of 2008. While the global recession caused a drop in prices as economic activity dropped, the recovery has witnessed a return to higher prices, and another commodity boom looks set to continue in the coming years.

To what extent was this boom caused or aggravated by outsourcing? The question relies heavily on the role of outsourcing in catalyzing growth in developing economies, particularly China, and the resulting effect of increased demand for commodities.

We'll take a look at this effect for each of the major categories of energy, metals and minerals, and agricultural commodities below.

Energy

The decade from 2000 represents an evolving picture in the impact that outsourcing as an industry has played and will play in influencing—albeit indirectly—global energy prices. We'll use China as a proxy for looking at this issue.

According to a study by the United States International Trade Commission, China's share of global crude petroleum consumption doubled from 4 percent to 8 percent between 1999 and 2004, and Chinese imports of crude oil increased 931 percent between 1999 and 2005.[49] The ITC study estimated that China's increased demand alone during this period was enough to have increased global oil prices by 12 to 37 percent from 1999 to 2004.[50]

However, during this same time, the price of oil increased from roughly $16/barrel in January 1999 to $55/barrel by the close of 2004, a surge of nearly 350 percent.[51] This implies that the entire impact of China's incremental demand was a relatively small cause of higher prices during this time period—*up until that point.*

In terms of coal, another major source of energy consumption, the World Bank reports that China's demand increased by 458 million tons between 2003 and 2007, which represented 18 percent of the total increase in global demand. However, China increased its own domestic production of coal by 421 million tons during this same period, effectively offsetting its increase in demand and contributing very little to overall global market tightness.[52]

Chinese demand for energy commodities, at least through 2005, had a relatively modest impact on global prices for oil and was negligible for coal.

There were other underlying causes that had more dramatic influence over the first half of the decade. A big factor in the 1990s was a sustained lack of investment in developing new supplies during a period of very low energy prices. Oil, at one point in the nineties, was just $10/barrel. It was not until the start of the 2000s that growing demand caught up with existing supply—and then started to exceed the supply base. Producers raced to bring on new sources. However, developing new oil or coal fields takes years.

In addition to the supply constraints, demand increased around the world across the spectrum for virtually all commodities, including energy, driven by economic growth in both developing and advanced economies.

Finally, in the case of oil, as market conditions tightened, there were a series of one-off factors that influenced prices, ranging from political volatility in producer countries to hurricanes in the US gulf region, which impacted production.

All of these factors, not just outsourcing, caused energy prices to begin increasing dramatically up until 2008 when the Great Recession struck. Economic growth in developing countries significantly influenced by the outsourcing industry was not the biggest factor.

However, that was then. This is now. The picture is changing rapidly.

In the case of oil, Chinese consumption may double over the next 20 years, from 7.7 million barrels per day to 15.3 million barrels per day, and Indian oil consumption will nearly double to 4.7 million barrels per day. A significant portion of the increased consumption will need to come from imports, meaning prices will go up around the world. As economies fully recover, higher prices are likely for everyone.[53]

Much the same story is occurring with coal. China currently produces 70 percent of its energy from coal-fired power plants and it is adding capacity rapidly (an estimated 500 gigawatts of new capacity over the next ten years—twice Japan's total current power generation capacity). These are huge numbers, and we are just seeing the early impacts now. In 2007 China swung decisively from being an exporter of coal to a net importer. In 2010 China may have imported 110 million tons of coal or more. The United States has even begun to export coal to China despite the great distance and cost of transportation. Now China is about to become the world's largest coal importer, beating out Japan in a development that emerged stunningly fast.[54] Asia overall may add enough capacity over the next three years to require an additional billion tons of coal annually. This will cause prices for everyone to increase as well.[55]

Growth in developing countries is only one of several reasons for increased energy prices up through the Great Recession, but that will not necessarily be true in the near future as global economic growth recovers. It is relatively safe to say that outsourcing, as an industry that has driven economic growth in economies like China, has had a relatively small, indirect impact on energy prices to date, but that this looks set to change dramatically in the coming years.

Metals

When it comes to the price of metal—the basic ingredient in building everything from cars to bridges, buildings to airplanes—growth in China has been a major driver in global price increases. According to the World Bank, between 1999 and 2005, "China accounted for nearly two-thirds of the growth in global demand (for metals), as its volume growth more than doubled."[56] Chinese demand has been particularly strong in metals and minerals such as copper, iron ore, lead, nickel, and zinc that have seen some of the biggest prices increases.

As manufacturing production shifted to China from around the world, China's use of metals increased dramatically, according to the World Bank, which measures how much metal goes into producing a unit of gross domestic product (GDP), or metal intensity. The global trend up until the mid 1990s was of steady decline in the metal intensity as countries found ways to become more efficient with metals in manufacturing and as developed economies shifted structurally toward more service-related activities. Then, in the mid-nineties, the trend reversed. The World Bank deemed this "almost entirely" due to the impact of China, where metal intensity was increasing rapidly. Metal intensity in China is now four times higher than in developed countries and twice as high as in other developing countries.[57] The World Bank specifically notes that the rapid increase in metal intensity was related to the shift of global manufacturing capacity from developing countries to China, e.g. outsourcing.

In theory, making a widget in America should require about the same amount of metals as making a widget in China. However, creating the supply chain to build those widgets has entailed building out all the factories that supply components going into the widgets, the factory that makes the widget, and the entire supporting infrastructure, from roads to ports. These activities are metal intensive until the infrastructure is in place.

As China grows, it is not just industrializing; it is also urbanizing. There is a corresponding boom in urban infrastructure and housing construction. All of this activity requires basic materials such as steel, cement, copper, and nickel. As China sucks in vast quantities of these materials to build its roads, ports, factories, and residential buildings, the prices for these materials increases around the world for everyone.

The beginning of the Great Recession saw prices fall back with economic activity, but they have recovered rapidly in late 2009 and through 2010 as economic growth stabilized in many countries.

What then is outsourcing's role in higher prices for metals? It seems fair to say that the outsourcing of manufacturing and services to countries like China and India plays a significant role directly in the goods it manufactures for exports as well as in catalyzing a larger domestic building boom in infrastructure, housing, and industrial production than would otherwise exist. The indirect cost of outsourcing is the higher prices for metals imposed on the global economy by developing countries', but primarily China's, rapid industrialization and urbanization.

Agriculture

Food commodity prices also jumped globally in 2007 and 2008, resulting in shortages for many, higher prices for all, and new hardships for people on the edge of poverty. In 2008, the number of people around the world facing malnourishment increased from 850 million to 1 billion as a result of these higher prices, reversing many of the gains from previous economic growth.

The increase in prices amounted to a 64 percent jump in real US dollar terms across all food types. However, this increase hid even larger swings among some basic commodities. Rice, for instance, jumped from below $400 per ton to nearly $1,000 at its peak as some supplier countries imposed export controls and importing countries raced to bid for alternatives.

To what extent was outsourcing indirectly causing these price increases through the boom in economic growth in countries such as China and India? The answer appears to be relatively little.

The International Fund for Agricultural Development (IFAD) noted, in a paper in 2008, six causal reasons for the run-up in food prices. The reasons range from a drop in supply due to bad weather in some countries, historically low buffer stock levels, increased energy prices that are highly correlated to agricultural goods (fertilizer prices tripled and transportation costs doubled in recent years due to higher petroleum prices), increased demand for biofuels, economic growth in developing countries such as China and India that increased demand for meat and cereal, and finally trade policies in some countries.[58]

Among the reasons outlined, growth and changing diets in developed countries from China to India to Brazil accounted for only part of the reason for increased food prices. The World Bank has even more recently suggested that the contribution from developing countries was not the biggest influence on prices, as grain demand did not accelerate for developing countries as a whole or for China despite increases in GDP. For instance, Chinese consumption of some grains like rice and wheat had actually declined.[59] While the role of economic growth in developing countries on food prices was relatively small, the World Bank finds that the impact of rising oil and fertilizer prices accounted for as much as 30 percent of the overall cost increases.[60]

The direct impact on food prices from economic growth in developing countries, driving higher demand for agricultural commodities and indirectly inspiring higher energy prices, is relatively modest, although not zero, based on the above.

Given that economic growth in developing countries is only a small portion of the cause and outsourcing is only one driver of economic growth in these countries, it can be assumed that there is very little cost that can be attributed to the outsourcing industry for the recent spikes in food prices for consumers in America as well as around the world.

Summary

The indirect impact of outsourcing due to economic growth in countries like China, India, and others has had a measurable, but relatively small impact on global energy prices up through 2008. In some sectors such as oil, it may have caused 5 to 10 percent of the increase in prices at their peak in 2008. In coal, there appears to have been a negligible impact. However, this picture is beginning to change dramatically for both oil and coal as global economic growth returns and the rapid increase in energy demand in China in particular and the rest of Asia continues to grow apace.

In the case of agricultural goods, there are a number of causes related to the recent run-up in prices that peaked in 2008. However, the indirect impact of outsourcing leading to increased demand in developing countries is a relatively minor portion of this so far. The bigger reasons relate to bad weather causing lower yields, increases in input prices, as well as diversion to biofuel production.

If the indirect impact of outsourcing on energy and food prices up to this point has been relatively small, the increase in metal prices is clearly not. Here the picture indicates the large price increases in metals and minerals were directly related to growth in China, primarily driven by the shift of manufacturing production from developed countries and its multiplier effect on infrastructure and housing.

Outsourcing, therefore, is linked to increases in metal and mineral prices from the early 2000s until 2008 and any inflation in prices that were passed on to US consumers and taxpayers during this time. It is also reasonable to expect near term increases in energy prices (yet to be quantified) in the next few years as global economic growth recovers around the globe and increased demand in Asia begins to draw more heavily on imports, thus increasing prices for all.

CHAPTER 7

Unfair Competition

IN MUCH OF THE literature about the stresses Americans are facing from offshore outsourcing specifically and globalization in general, a consistent theme emerges: China is competing unfairly. China's outsized impact on global exports and the outsourcing industry as a whole means the allegation of unfair competition deserves some attention and analysis in the context of how much outsourcing is responsible for any negative impacts. There is much less focus on India because it has a floating currency, which is set by market forces rather than government restrictions, and its trade surplus with the United States is relatively modest. There is little sense that India is competing unfairly. China is a different story.

In general, I divide the accusation of China's unfair competition into two parts. The first is the China Price, the fact that China is able to offer the lowest price for any manufactured product and is thus unfairly taking jobs from Americans. The second factor, complementing the China Price, is an undervalued currency, which forms one of the foundation planks in the China Price, making exports unfairly attractive. Both will be briefly examined to determine if outsourcing as an industry has contributed to or wholly created these issues.

The China Price

Critics have long cited the China Price as an unfair advantage in trade. What they mean is that China has an unfair combination of cheap labor, lax enforcement of environmental and labor laws that make exporting more attractive than other places, and a pervasive web of subsidies and government incentives that encourage exports over domestic consumption. Much of this is true, but needs to be put in context.

Cheap labor is one of the main ingredients cited in the China Price. It is certainly true that labor in China is cheaper than labor in the United States. However, even five years ago, Chinese manufacturing wages were averaging $250 to $350 per month along the eastern coast, where most manufacturing takes place. At the same time, Indonesia, the Philippines, and all but the most expensive locations in Thailand recorded significantly lower manufacturing wages at $100 to $200 per month. Up until the recent economic crisis, the gap was getting bigger as wages in China grew at two to three times the rate of the rest of Southeast Asia.[61]

The Great Recession did not reverse this trend. In fact, after an initial pause, the trends returned in 2010. Acute labor shortages have been reported in China's Guangdong province, commonly called the "workshop of the world."[62] Recent labor strikes for better wages (at Honda factories and others) have been highly publicized as have scandals over working conditions (including Foxconn). All of these forces are combining to exert upward pressure on wages for Chinese workers. Foxconn, for instance, doubled its pay across the board as part of its response to the crisis, though it then started talking about moving factories inland where labor is 30 percent cheaper. Foxconn's decision to increase wages may represent a watershed moment in rising labor costs in China.

Wage pressures are rising. Underlying demographic changes foretell a growing scarcity of workers in China, which is already adding to these wage pressures, both for workers along the Chinese coast as well as in the interior. The gap in wages between China and the rest of developing Asia looks set to grow wider. Cheap labor, therefore, is apparently not the only factor in the China Price, for labor is cheaper elsewhere and getting more expensive in China.

Lax regulation and enforcement is another element cited in the China Price, and there is certainly merit here. Although China has put in place extensive new labor laws requiring employee contracts and mandating overtime, resulting in workers suing for their rights, enforcement by local authorities remains generally lax. At least one survey has found that just 60 percent of workers are covered by employee contracts, despite the law's requirements.[63]

While the labor rights picture in China appears to be improving slowly, it is clear that lax regulation and enforcement remain consistent problems. However, it is not clear that regulatory enforcement is any stricter in other poor, developing countries seeking to attract jobs.

The third element is the pervasive web of Chinese government subsidies and incentives to build manufacturing in China. One recent example highlighted how China has stolen a lead in clean-energy technologies—precisely the industry that Western politicians like to highlight as a future job bank. What has happened, however, is that China has quickly gone from being a minor producer of solar panels and wind turbines to making nearly half of the world's output of each within a few short years.

A *New York Times* article describes the help one local Chinese province provided to a new solar panel maker, Hunan Sunzone Optoelectronics.[64] The web of state support includes the full range of land transfers (essentially giving land for free or at greatly reduced rates, creating an instant asset for a new company), low-interest loans combined with direct-interest subsidies by local government (making borrowing ultra low cost), streamlined permitting that takes months instead of years, and local market protection (local content rules to protect domestic producers). The list goes on and on, and much of it appears to be in direct contradiction to World Trade Organization (WTO) restrictions which prohibits things like unfair subsidies.

Perhaps the most telling anecdote is how the state-owned bankers come out to the factory to offer the owner help. Excluding sub-prime mortgages, when was the last time you saw a banker do a house call to the borrower in the United States?

Despite all of these advantages from cheap labor to all-encompassing government support, the China Price does not appear to be invincible. In the last several years, tens of thousands of factories in low-end, labor-intensive industries have been closing in the coastal regions of China and either moving inland or relocating to cheaper countries such as Vietnam, Bangladesh, or India. In the electronics industry, production is forecast to be increasingly targeted toward India. One study estimated that Indian manufacturing will come on stream and capture much of the future growth in electronics contract manufacturing.[65] Thus the perception of China as a single, monolithic producer for all manufacturing as a result of an invincible China Price is beginning to change and will likely continue to do so.

In her book, *The China Price*, Alexandra Harney notes that before there was a China Price, there was a Japan Price, a Hong Kong price, a Taiwan Price, and a Mexico Price.[66] This emphasizes the fact that the China Price is temporary.

It is hard to conclude that the China Price is a conspiracy built on labor that is cheaper than anywhere else or regulations less strictly enforced. There is a very strong case, however, that a pervasive set of government subsidies and support ranging from land transfers to subsidized loans directly promotes the building of factories in China and keeps costs artificially low. This is clearly unfair both in the spirit and letter of the WTO.

But this isn't the whole story. Manufacturing's rush to China over the last twenty years was also aided by a series of fair competitive moves by China, including smart policies such as special economic and free trade zones, and smart investments ranging from roads to ports. It has also been aided by advances in technology (cheaper communications) and transportation (intermodal cargo). Companies have been drawn not just by these policies (fair and unfair) but also by the prospect of a vast market in China and an agglomeration of similar industries that found it equally easy to set up business and start producing. Outsourcing did not create all of these conditions initially in China—or any other country— but it did reinforce them once a virtuous circle had begun.

Nor is the story just about government. Chinese suppliers and entrepreneurs have not stood still when it comes to competing for business from Western customers, a factor not fully appreciated by many people. A study by the Conference Board found that Chinese firms had achieved an "astounding" level of productivity gains, on the order of 20.4 percent annually between 1995 and 2003 (3 percent is considered good in a developed economy like the United States). Astounding is no exaggeration in this case. What productivity gains this high mean is that Chinese firms are sprinting to be better, cheaper, and faster suppliers to their customers. The rate of turnover of firms and the allocation and reallocation of labor in China was also found to be roughly on par with labor flows in the United States. This strongly suggests that Chinese firms are competing and innovating rapidly to win business. Companies that are not good are failing. New ones are rising to take their place. This rapid churn and intensive competition represent values we traditionally associate as fair in our own economy.[67]

The idea that a China Price is built on cheap labor and lax regulation is not entirely accurate. Cheap labor is not unique to China, and it is not proven that other developing countries are any more stringent on enforcement. However, China does provide a pervasive set of government subsidies and support that encourages companies to move production to China, and this type of government support is clearly unfair in its breadth and depth.

But what's outsourcing's role and responsibility in all this? It is clear that outsourcing as an industry gravitates to locations where production is efficient, cost effective, competitive, and concentrated and that this process can be a self-reinforcing cycle if it works well. In the case of China and the China Price, this is clearly happening on a large scale, and some elements are fair while others are not.

Currency

The other leg of the unfair competition story is the accusation that China's currency, the yuan, is intentionally undervalued in a mercantilist policy to gain trade at the expense of its neighbors. Politicians and pundits have long been convinced that this is the case, but economists have been less sure.

In fact, estimates of how much the Chinese currency was undervalued ranged between 0 and 50 percent during the early and mid 2000s.[68] The debate was loudest when China's currency was fixed at 8.25 to the US dollar. After China established a managed float in 2005, the currency appreciated until 2008 to 6.83, a gain of over 20 percent. This appreciation accounts for a large part of the revaluation that critics were initially calling for. However, it did not result in a reversal of trade imbalances. They kept growing.

In the midst of the Great Recession and the rapid drop in economic activity, China froze the exchange rate at 6.83 as an emergency measure, and it stayed there until June 2010, when it began a managed float again after a great deal of criticism and political pressure. By May 2010, one study estimated that the yuan was still 24 percent undervalued relative to the US dollar, but down from earlier estimates of as much as 40 percent.[69]

More recently in June 2011, an article in the *Wall Street Journal* argued that the yuan might be getting closer to fair value. It pointed out that China's trade surplus and current-account surplus had declined dramatically. China's current account surplus in 2010 was 5.2 percent, just half of what it had been three years earlier in 2007. With surpluses going down, the implication is that the yuan may not be as grossly undervalued as it once was.[70]

However you cut it, it would seem obvious that China is a currency manipulator, even though this is a politically loaded term. That fact that it sets (by government fiat) its currency rate rather than allowing it to fluctuate by a market float seems to make this obvious.

The Chinese currency is in all likelihood undervalued. If the currency is allowed to continue appreciating, then it might well suppress Chinese exports or encourage US imports to a point that eliminates the trade imbalance.

Or it may not. The history of exchange rates and trade deficits with Japan offer a counterpoint to consider. In the early 1980s, the Japanese yen was in the range of 250 to 300 yen per US dollar. After the 1985 Plaza Accords agreed to adjust currency rates to equalize the market, the yen appreciated to 150 to the dollar, and it has steadily risen since, reaching a level of nearly 77 yen to the dollar in September 2011. Japan has had a trade surplus with the United States most if not the entire time.

Exchange rates have an influence, but are not the only factor in determining trade flows and competition between countries. The bigger question is to what extent outsourcing as an industry is responsible for an unfair Chinese exchange rate. In practical terms, the answer seems to be little to none, but that is not to say that the industry is without blame.

The industry clearly responds to exchange rates and economic signals provided by governments and economies around the world. It lobbies for its self-interest. The industry will quickly move to exploit economic advantage wherever it finds it. However, the exchange rate for the Chinese currency is set by the Chinese government, which does so by internal calculations and within a framework of international relations, agreements, and political economic considerations.

Regardless of the role of currency in unfair trade balances and flows, currency policies are set by governments. The outsourcing industry will lobby for favorable exchange rates, and it will respond to fluctuations in exchange rates, but ultimately it does not set them.

Summary

China competes both fairly and unfairly—fairly with smart policies and investments, unfairly with subsidies, support, and unfair exchange rates. Yet the moral cost of moving jobs to lower-cost countries is already well covered in the sections on job loss and wage stagnation. The injustice toward those workers is covered in the section on labor exploitation. A country's factor inputs (cheap labor, cheap land) are not influenced by any industry. Nor is a currency valuation by a sovereign government set by multinationals.

The debate around the China Price, fair and unfair trade policies, and China's exchange rate are good and important debates to have, but I have not found any incremental moral cost of outsourcing related to China's fair and unfair competition for trade that adds to the existing discussion in this book.

CHAPTER 8

Buying America

MANY COUNTRIES HAVE benefited directly and indirectly from outsourcing and outsourcing has directly led to their accumulating wealth in the form of foreign currency reserves—currencies other than their own that they hold in reserve as savings, if you will. This chapter explores how these foreign reserves are used to buy American assets and their direct and indirect costs to America as a result of the outsourcing industry.

Sovereign Wealth

There are two primary sources of sovereign wealth that can be directly and indirectly related to outsourcing. Directly, many countries have accumulated wealth as a result of trade surpluses, a good portion of which is related to outsourcing. Indirectly, economic growth has inspired higher energy and commodity prices, and this has led to the rise, in particular, of petrodollar wealth in oil-producing countries from the Middle East to Russia.

All told, petrodollar countries and Asian countries accumulated $8.5 trillion up through the end of 2007.[71] Much of this wealth was held by central banks, many of which, including China, used the accumulated foreign currency reserves to purchase US Treasury Bills. Another portion of this wealth was invested via sovereign wealth funds (SWFs) into stocks. SWFs are state-owned investment funds that purchase equity shares. They have spurred a great deal of fear in some circles over concerns that they might use their wealth and power to pursue political, rather than purely business and economic, goals. The numbers involved in both foreign exchange holdings and SWFs are enormous. By mid-2011 China alone had an estimated $3 trillion in reserves. Asian SWFs—from Singapore's

Temasek to China Investment Corp (CIC)—had roughly $700 billion to invest by the start of 2008, prior to the Great Recession.

The question becomes: was this accumulated wealth used in any way that resulted in a real or potential cost or threat to America and its citizens?

In the case of Treasury Bill purchases, the net result was to lower the cost of credit for American consumers in everything from car loans to home mortgages to credit cards. This undoubtedly has saved, and continues to save, American households hundreds of dollars or more each year. One of the biggest fears, however, is that China's vast purchases of Treasury Bills will mean they are able to exercise undue influence over US policies as America's biggest creditor.

There appears to be little evidence that this has occurred. In fact, these fears seem ironic in light of recent events. On the one hand, economist and columnist Paul Krugman refers to China's accumulation of US Treasury Bills as "China's Dollar Trap" and suggests that the Chinese leadership didn't have a real plan in mind when they bought US Treasury Bills. Instead, they have a real problem now. They have built up huge holdings of US Treasury Bills at precisely the time when imbalances in the global economy must eventually be resolved by a devaluation of the US dollar.[72] This will result in huge losses for China's dollar holdings.

Purchasing Treasury Bills was seen as a safe investment and an asset held in trust for the future of the Chinese people. China has now awoken to the possibility that it might lose substantial sums of money when the dollar devalues. Here's a ballpark estimate: China could lose over $200 billion. That's based on the view that China has about $1.2 trillion in Treasury Bills, that these are long-term holdings, and that total appreciation of the yuan over time reaches 20 percent.

Attempts by the Chinese to diversify their holdings away from dollars into Euros in 2010 were largely unsuccessful due a series of economic crises in Europe, which resulted in the financial bailouts of Greece, Ireland, and Portugal with further instability possible in more countries. Suddenly the Euro looked less safe than the US dollar.

As if this wasn't bad enough, China's SWFs reflected enormous losses on paper for equity investments made during the Great Recession. Chinese leadership began seriously diversifying in 2007 on the very eve of the economic crisis, a monumentally bad stroke of fortune. One Chinese SWF invested an estimated $160 billion in foreign, primarily US, equities. By early 2009, these investments had lost more than half their value, some $80 billion in losses.[73] However, these were paper losses and will have been recouped if these equities were held through 2011 rather than sold.

To the Chinese, investments in Treasury Bills or US equities can hardly look like a sound investment. Billions of dollars are at risk, and hundreds of billions more are almost certain to be lost in the future as China's currency appreciates. The Chinese public is reportedly outraged and believes the country was conned into buying these assets.[74]

From an American perspective, however, it is hard to see what cost is imposed on America as a result of these investments. At key junctures in the economic crisis, Chinese SWFs made strategic investments in numerous US financial companies (as did other nations), a significant benefit for Americans. American consumers continue to benefit from low interest rates, underwritten in part by ongoing Chinese purchases of American debt.

The storyline on sovereign wealth and SWFs is likely to continue evolving. At this juncture, it appears that fears in some quarters of the United States have proven to be mostly unfounded. Rather than exercise power over US decision making, sovereign wealth investments will almost certainly face large losses on dollar-denominated assets in the future. In the meantime, the continued purchase of Treasury Bills by Chinese and other countries simply results in lower interest rates in the United States, creating more favorable conditions for US businesses and consumers.

Not everything is rosy in this scenario, and I do not wish to suggest that the continued flow of overseas financing of America's debt is entirely a good thing. There is a risk of future insolvency in the United States if we don't grapple with our deficits and accumulating debt. But these are political and fiscal policy decisions that are made at home, completely independent of the outsourcing industry. Outsourcing is not to blame if we as a nation simply haven't the will to balance our own budget.

Buying US Companies

State-controlled wealth is not the only source of investment in the United States. We may soon see an onslaught from the private sector as Chinese and Indian businesses buy up companies and brands to gain access to markets and technology.

Before the economic crisis, nearly 90 percent of Chinese companies surveyed indicated they were seeking to merge or acquire in Asia, Europe, or North America in the next twelve months.[75] The Great Recession and recent losses by national SWFs may have tempered some of this zeal, but at some point, these firms are coming to our shores in large numbers.

For some, this is frightening stuff. But it is not new. In the eighties, Japan was widely perceived to be buying up America, and highly visible acquisitions such as the Rockefeller Center fed our insecurity and fear of failure. Yet within a few short years of popular movies like *Rising Sun*, the Japanese economy imploded and entered a decade of stagnation. Meanwhile, the American economy grew rapidly while riding booms in Internet and e-commerce, telecom and biotech, and more.

Almost no one worries about Japan now—other than companies like Toyota (albeit less so after recent quality issues) and Honda. Nor is the foreign purchase of companies in America necessarily a bad thing. It's expensive to buy and shut down a company just to get access to technology (foreign companies have been, and will most likely continue to be, barred from buying strategic or defense oriented companies). Since many of the new entrants won't have existing US distribution, service, and maintenance capabilities, it probably means they will keep assets, jobs, and American employees in place. Ironically, this might mean a foreign purchase results in *more* job security for Americans than if these companies were bought by a comparable US company that then focused on cost savings through consolidation.

The moral cost of all this is yet to be determined. It could result in needed investment in America and more jobs here. It could also result in the manipulation of our companies and financial markets and in the theft of our technology.

Summary

There are legitimate reasons to be concerned about the rising financial powers of some developing countries and whether they will use this power to influence or purchase assets in America and abroad. Outsourcing as an industry has had both a direct and indirect role in creating the wealth and foreign exchange that have led to this accumulation of financial power. However, the costs and fears about foreign purchases of US assets seem largely exaggerated, whereas the benefits are tangible and come in the form of reduced interest rates for Americans across various categories of debt.

A reasonable conclusion is that there are legitimate issues to be worried about the growing financial power of some countries, but there is little or no additional moral cost to America at this point caused by the outsourcing industry either directly or indirectly as a result of sovereign wealth funds and the purchase of American assets.

Chapter 9

Geopolitical Impacts

ONE OF THE BIGGEST CHALLENGES for America over the next generation will be to manage the rise of new powers in the global economy, including China, India, and a group of less savory characters—the petro-tyrants.

Nothing illustrates this more than the G7 group of economies. Founded in the 1970s, the original G7 was composed of the United States, Japan, Germany, the United Kingdom, France, Italy, and Canada. These countries were the largest free-market economies of their era and, combined, they had an enormous influence on the global economy. They could set the rules for everyone. No longer. The G7 is increasingly a relic of the past.

Today, if you were to pick the seven largest economies, you would have, in order by size: the United States, China, Japan, Germany, France, the United Kingdom, and Brazil (some suggest Brazil has catapulted to fifth). India is currently tenth but will soon take the ninth spot from Canada and may continue marching up the ranks if growth is maintained in the range of 8 to 10 percent per year.

As the old G7 has lost power, it has been replaced by a larger and more unwieldy G20 comprising the top twenty economies in the world including all of the former G7 as well as countries like China, India, Brazil, Russia, and more. The challenge has been that this larger group is having a much harder time finding consensus on how to run the global economy.

Outsourcing has an indirect role in these rapid changes in global geopolitics. It has been the primary mechanism fueling economic growth in China and India (notwithstanding the economic crisis of 2008 to 2010), which has supported the rise of these new powers and changes in the global power balance. Following is a very brief survey of some of the key challenges outsourcing has introduced to geopolitics.

China Rising

No development on the geopolitical stage is more significant than the rise of China. This rise inspires nothing less than awe and dread across a broad swath of the political spectrum in America and elsewhere.

China's growing economic might is indisputable. It now holds $3 trillion in foreign reserves, enough to buy a country or two. China gives more loans to the developing world than the World Bank, and it invests more in the developing world than the US. China's political influence is rising in proportion to this economic weight. China has the power to undermine the global consensus on any issue, and it is forming its own coalitions and pursing its own agenda.

There are military implications as well. China is now making stealth fighters and planning to build aircraft carriers. A significant challenger to American power and dominance in the East could well be on the horizon. America's foreign policy establishment is abuzz with the implications of the challenge. *Foreign Affairs* magazine has run a series of articles under banners like "The China Challenge" (May/June 2009) and "Will China's Rise Lead to War?" (March/April 2011).

China's rise is a central challenge for America and the world. What's less talked about is that exports continue to be the engine through which China has accumulated wealth, catalyzed economic growth, and accrued both economic and political sway. These exports are almost entirely the result of the outsourcing industry moving production to China. The outsourcing industry bears significant responsibility for the rise of China as a new economic and political power. Put another way, without the widespread movement of the outsourcing industry to China over the last two decades, the Chinese economy would be a fraction of the size it is today and China would have a correspondingly smaller influence on global affairs than it does as a result.

The New Petro-Tyrants: Venezuela and Iran

Outsourcing fuels economic growth around the world, which in turn, increases demand for energy (despite short-term changes in demand and price caused during the Great Recession and its ongoing recovery). This has led to the unintended moral consequence of rising oil prices empowering a new generation of petro-tyrants who pursue interests that are anti-American.

Venezuela and Iran are the two most prominent examples of anti-American regimes that profit from higher oil prices. Under Hugo Chavez, Venezuela has used its oil profits to fund leftist causes throughout Latin America. Iran has used its own oil income to finance terrorism abroad and (almost certainly) to attempt developing nuclear weapons at home. However, in recent years both regimes have been forced to struggle with severely constrained budgets for their domestic and foreign agendas in part because of fluctuations in energy prices and in part due to economic mismanagement. And, coincidentally, both regimes have encountered electoral challenges at home. Iran's regime continues to face a crisis of legitimacy among its own people after an election that was widely considered fraudulent.

While these countries are a thorn in the side for US interests, what's also true is that the relationship between outsourcing and higher oil prices has been relatively weak until now. Neither the rise nor the fall of anti-Americanism in Iran or Venezuela can be attributed as a significant direct or indirect cost of outsourcing.

Russia: The New Energy Superpower

Russia is another power that has regained a measure of strength and confidence due to higher oil prices. The increased wealth from oil has given Russia the chance to regain some of its strength since the fall of the Soviet Bloc, and the government has used this newfound wealth in a series of increasingly authoritarian restrictions at home and aggressive actions abroad. These range from the invasion of Georgia to the cutting off of natural gas supplies to Europe over payment disputes with Ukraine.

Despite the strained nature of the relationship between Russia and the West (recently on the mend in 2010 and 2011), the resurgence of Russia (and its tribulations after the fall in oil prices and subsequent rebound) and its use of power cannot be directly or indirectly attributed as a cost of outsourcing. The link between higher energy prices and outsourcing, as noted earlier, is relatively weak to date, although this may start to change in the near future.

India

Finally there is India. India is in many respects the epitome of what we would like to see in the world—it is a large, friendly democracy following the American economic model, or at least generally reforming in that direction. We traditionally don't see fellow democracies as threats. We have even backed India for a permanent seat on the UN Security Council. But India's interests will not always align with America's, whether they relate to free trade, foreign policy, or ethical behavior. India is also pushing to have a larger stake in world decision making whether that is via the United Nations or through the increasingly important G20.

Given the importance of outsourcing to India's economy—which is nearing 6.4 percent of GDP in 2011 and increased foreign reserves by 36 percent as of 2010—outsourcing is clearly a significant factor in India's rise to prominence.

Summary

The world is changing. Outsourcing and the consequent flow of manufacturing and services jobs to developing countries such as China, India, and Eastern Europe has dramatically accelerated growth in these regions, fueling a development boom that has increased both their economic and political power on the world stage.

Many of these developments are very positive. But not all. Relatively speaking, America's power is declining as that of other countries rises. Significant challenges will emerge as a result, the least of which being disagreements with other countries regarding policies and approaches to global issues and relations.

Where there are negative impacts (direct or indirect), then these impacts should be accounted for as a moral cost of outsourcing. Yet it may also be that the more countries are engaged in the global economic system, the more they have a stake in its success. If this is true, then outsourcing also has a beneficial impact that may offset the costs in part or whole.

CHAPTER 10

Global Imbalances

CURRENT ACCOUNT IMBALANCES between major economies have been in the news a lot over the last several years. Imbalances are caused when some countries run big current account surpluses and, on the flip side, when other countries run big current account deficits. These imbalances create systemic risks for the global economy because, eventually, imbalances have to adjust. The adjustments can be gradual and ordered, or they can be sudden, chaotic, and harmful.

Two of the biggest sources of the current imbalances in the global economy are China's surplus and the United States' deficit. But there are others as well, including Germany's surplus with the rest of the European Union, and Japan's surplus with the rest of the world. Spain has been another example of a country with a large current account deficit.

At the November 2010 G20 Summit in Seoul, global imbalances were at the top of the agenda and led to much discussion and disagreement. The meeting concluded without a successful plan to address the issue.

In the case of China, outsourcing has played a significant role in generating the imbalance. China has pursued an export-led strategy that has seen a vast surge in net exports as a percentage of GDP, in the range of 40 to 45 percent in recent years. This has made China a huge surplus country that sucks in vast amounts of foreign exchange, which the country then uses to finance the primary debtor countries, namely the United States.

It is clear that China's surplus imbalance is primarily related to outsourcing, which has acted as a vehicle for moving production to China and underpinned Chinese economic growth. Outsourcing is not wholly to blame, however. Chinese policies ranging from export subsidies to an excessive internal system of rewards favoring economic growth and exports have helped drive the focus of the Chinese economy in attracting outsourced production.

The German situation is somewhat different. Germany's massive current account surpluses are not driven by outsourcing at all but by a lack of domestic demand to pull in imports to balance the country's highly efficient and competitive export sector. Germany sees itself as having made the adjustments to be competitive and does not feel it is to blame. Across Europe, many other countries are bitter about the situation. Germany runs large current account surpluses and is a major contributor to global imbalances as well as political tensions within the European Union.

Japan is another current account surplus country that, like Germany, is highly successful at exporting but does not have strong enough domestic demand to balance its economy.

The responsibility of the surplus countries and the industries that enable them match the responsibility of the deficit countries in creating the problem. In this, the United States has a special burden that has nothing to do with outsourcing. US monetary and fiscal policies on taxation, consumption, and interest rates have all had a hand in encouraging large structural deficits in the US current account balance. In other words, our policies and politics encourage consumption over savings and we don't want to pay taxes, resulting in large deficits that have to be financed by money from other countries.

Imbalances are serious. By definition, they cannot go on forever. Adjustment often comes in the shape of an economic crisis resulting in lost jobs and deep recession. Outsourcing as an industry is partly responsible for the accumulated problem of global economic balances on the surplus side (mostly in the case of China). It is much less so for the deficit side (US).

CONCLUSION

OFFSHORE OUTSOURCING HAS a moral cost related to American jobs, communities, and individuals. Part I of this book has focused on documenting these costs. While it is not always easy to quantify them on purely moral grounds, the intent has been to put them into a political and economic context so that a moral analysis can be constructed.

These costs from outsourcing come in a variety of shapes and forms. They manifest themselves both directly and indirectly. Some are obvious; others require extrapolation. The list includes job loss but extends beyond that with wage stagnation and middle-class anxiety as well as a host of indirect costs.

Here is a brief summary of what we have covered:

We have estimated that 450,000 to 550,000 jobs may be lost annually due to outsourcing. This represents just 2 to 2.5 percent of total annual job losses from layoffs and separations for all reasons across the United States—the other 98 percent of job losses are caused by factors other than outsourcing. Regardless of the low percentage, the number is significant, and job loss is devastating to individuals and their communities.

We have found that—aside from the job loss aspect—there is a relatively weak relationship between outsourcing as an industry and the tangible causes of middle-class anxiety and fears for the American Dream. Middle-class anxiety is heavily linked to wage stagnation on the one hand and rising costs on the other, especially of public services such as health care and education. Outsourcing appears to have a weak correlation—at least since 2000—to wage stagnation and little or no relationship to the steep increases in health care and education costs, sectors that can neither be outsourced nor achieve productivity gains.

We have found that outsourcing, primarily in manufacturing, is systemically responsible for labor exploitation, environmental damage, and imports of bad, even dangerous, products into the United States. In each of these areas, outsourcing contributes significantly to the problem. Governments in both producing and destination countries also have significant responsibilities in this area and appear to have been equally remiss in enforcing existing regulations or developing sufficient capabilities to monitor trade flows and labor rights.

Outsourcing has very little causal linkage to price increases for energy and food commodities (at least until recently, and this picture may change dramatically as the global economic recovery gains pace). It is, however, closely related to metal and mineral price increases, which have resulted in higher costs for Americans in everything from cars to infrastructure.

There are several components of unfair competition, such as the China Price and exchange rates, for which outsourcing has very little direct responsibility. However, as an industry it responds to these pricing signals and gravitates to locations where they are the most favorable. Therefore, the industry bears some responsibility for their impact on America and American workers.

In the realm of geopolitics, it is not fair to lay blame to an industry that has very little to do with setting the foreign policies of host nations. While outsourcing has had a direct role in the growth of new powers such as China and India, it may also be that the countries most deeply embedded in the global economy and gaining the most benefit are also the most likely to act responsibly and in a restrained manner. If this is true, then outsourcing's role in this is not a cost.

Finally, in the case of global economic imbalances, outsourcing clearly plays a role on the surplus side of the equation by helping countries accumulate an imbalance in the first place. In this case, outsourcing helps to amplify both the size of the imbalance and the size of the crisis resulting from an adjustment. Said adjustments may cause a great deal of harm to people around the world.

This then is the summary of costs that we have identified that are caused either directly or indirectly by outsourcing as an industry. The goal of this section has been to catalog the largest moral costs from offshore outsourcing and to establish a framework of these moral costs. The costs identified here may not be the only ones. Every reader can look at them differently and bring fresh insights and new data to the problem. This catalog of costs will now be balanced against a similar analysis of benefits to follow. Both the costs and the benefits can then be weighed to develop a moral analysis and identify the net impact of outsourcing: good, bad, or ugly.

PART 2

BENEFITS

OVERVIEW

OUTSOURCING IMPOSES social and economic costs on America. This much is clear from the preceding part of this book. What is sometimes less popular to highlight, but no less true, is that America benefits from offshore outsourcing as well.

Most of the business literature focuses on cost savings, flexibility, access to global talent, and the profit gains for companies and their shareholders. But this is the business case. It's not the moral case, which requires looking more broadly at the social and political impacts of outsourcing. Business executives tread lightly in the debate over outsourcing for obvious reasons; courting controversy is not a career-enhancing move. Yet the social and political dimensions are precisely the ones that need the most explanation and dialogue.

Outsourcing results in cheaper products and better service. It increases corporate profits, which can be used to benefit shareholders, employees, and future retirees that own 401(k) accounts. It can be a tool to help save companies from failing and therefore salvage jobs. And, contrary to popular opinion, the United States has long been the beneficiary of jobs outsourced to America by foreign companies.

These are all substantial benefits of outsourcing. But critics—and advocates—err in stopping at the simple cases above. There are also benefits from the growth of destination countries like China and India that extend all the way back to our own shores with positive feedbacks that impact American wages, jobs, and opportunities.

The goal of this chapter is to look at how Americans benefit directly and indirectly from offshore outsourcing. The place to start is with the products we buy.

CHAPTER 11

Cheaper Goods

AN OBVIOUS BENEFIT of outsourcing production to countries like China is that American consumers gain the benefit of lower prices for everything from clothing to electronics, automobiles to toys. In broad terms, we can quantify this benefit.

The Peterson Institute of International Economics has calculated the cost savings to US consumers from global trade *as a whole* as being in the range of $2,800 to $5,000 for the average consumer and between $7,100 and $12,900 for the average household. That's roughly $1 trillion each year in savings for the economy in aggregate. Outsourcing is a subset of trade, and cheaper prices are only one aspect. This number, therefore, tops the range of the potential benefit of outsourcing specifically.[1]

A study by IHS Global Insight measures the impact that Walmart alone has had on consumer prices in the United States, and this study gets us closer to a number for outsourcing. The study—financed by Walmart—documents the impact that Walmart has had on reducing consumer prices in the United States and quantifies the benefits at the individual and household levels. Because Walmart relies heavily on a supply chain that utilizes suppliers located in China, the study is a good proxy for the impact one company's use of outsourcing has had on prices for US consumers.

The study finds that in 2006, Walmart saved consumers $287 billion due to the impact it had on reducing consumer price inflation over the last twenty years. This works out to $957 for each American and $2,500 for every household.[2]

But Walmart is just one example of the large, sophisticated retail chains that have proliferated across America. The Home Depot, Best Buy, Staples, Office Depot, Bed Bath & Beyond, Pier 1, Gap, Costco—

the list goes on and on and on. Name a category and there is a big box retailer that focuses on it, has hundreds if not thousands of stores, and uses global sourcing from suppliers in low-cost locations (often, but not always, China) paired up with sophisticated supply chain planning and information technology to deliver rock-bottom prices to American consumers.

To people on any budget, $1,000 is a big deal. At every income, price point, and quality level, we all shop to some extent at retailers—online, downtown, or by mail—that make some use of offshore production.

Cheaper products are one tangible benefit of outsourcing, even as the quality of the goods must be closely monitored. The true cost savings to American consumers from outsourcing lies somewhere between the IHS Global Insight study on the Walmart effect (which focuses on one large company with spillover effects throughout the economy) and the Peterson Institute's analysis of the benefits of trade as a whole. To err on the conservative side, we'll use the Walmart study as a baseline for the benefit of cheaper products as being roughly $1,000 for each American or $2,500 for every household in America.

CHAPTER 12
_____

Better Service

AMERICA IS AN ECONOMY largely driven by services, and services have fundamentally changed because of offshoring. Not only has 24-7 service become ubiquitous, but we also expect every business to have a call center and agents able and willing to spend the time talking us through every-thing from a billing error to a hard drive crash at any time of the day or night. Business has transformed the service experience by leveraging a global workforce.

Twenty-four-hour customer support is just one example. It can also be seen in the increasing speed by which many of our transactions are processed.

Consider these two contrasting realities: purchasing a passport from the United States Government and applying for a credit card by mail. You apply for both by mail, but the passport costs $110 and reportedly takes four to six weeks to process unless you pay a premium for expedited service. The credit card application is shipped by overnight carrier to an offshore processing center where the data is entered and processed within a few working days. You get your new credit card in the mail practically by the end of the week.

The comparison is not apples to apples in terms of the processes that must be followed—thankfully the US Government doesn't hand out passports the way financial services companies do credit cards—but the point is illustrative: service is faster and cheaper when it is outsourced to organizations that are more efficient and productive. It is also less expensive via global sourcing —which the US Government is not allowed to use.

So is there truly a moral benefit in outsourcing services? The answer, I think, is yes, but in a subtle way. Like it or not, life has sped up. Americans are forced to cope by working longer hours and with harder workloads, and in America today, it takes two incomes to make ends meet in most households. With both spouses working, the free time left for spending time with family, running errands, or calling customer service lines is increasingly limited. Furthermore, in today's cubicle-laden workspaces, the privacy to make a call during business hours to discuss the check you just bounced is wholly missing. What's left are nights and weekends. The evening hours after the kids are asleep have become the last free hours left for personal business, and fortunately twenty-four-hour service centers accommodate this need. However, these centers would be rare and expensive without offshore outsourcing.

As customers, we may rail against the foreign accent or the scripted response inherent in offshored call centers. Not every call is successful or enjoyable (or even intelligible). The quality of the service can always improve. But there is a bigger point. A generation ago, only the most high-end consumers would have had the ability or choice to simply pick up the phone and talk to their companies outside standard business hours. We now take this for granted.

The moral benefit in being able to access our banks, insurance companies, utilities, and health care companies at any hour of the day lies in the flexibility we have to use our time as we choose. The cost savings— both for employees and employers—are measured in the time off work that we don't have to take to get some of these chores done. Convenience and flexibility are significant benefits of outsourcing that Americans enjoy, even if it is not clear how to quantify this particular benefit.

CHAPTER 13

Insourcing

THE LARGELY UNHERALDED story of jobs created in the United States by foreign companies insourcing their business here is an economic and social benefit that deserves examination. According to the Organization for International Investment, approximately 5.5 million Americans are employed by the US subsidiaries of foreign companies as of 2009. These are the jobs that have been outsourced to the United States from other countries. It's been happening for so long that we take it for granted, and the numbers are huge.

Foreign companies support an annual payroll of nearly $403 billion, an average of $73,124 per US employee. That average is 34.7 percent higher than the average compensation paid by US companies at home. Foreign companies not only create jobs in the United States to produce for the domestic market here, but their US subsidiaries also account for nearly 19 percent of all US manufacturing exports (more than $215 billion) each year. Furthermore, foreign companies spend nearly $40 billion annually on research and development in the United States (up from $34 billion in 2009), employing tens of thousands of highly paid engineers, scientists, designers, and other high-skill workers.[3] These companies are primarily from developed countries such as those in Europe and Japan. Japanese companies, for instance, now employ nearly 700,000 Americans after a generation of investing in the United States.[4]

The debate about outsourcing tends to focus exclusively on the jobs lost in the United States. The key point, however, is that outsourcing is a two-way street. Many millions of jobs—on average higher paying and more highly skilled jobs—have been created in America by companies moving production and operations here. Future waves of investment are projected to filter in from China, India, and others. They come for a variety of reasons ranging from suppliers seeking to build closer to their customers, companies seeking to gain access to technology, and businesses that seek to employ workers at the top end of the highly skilled and talented American workforce.

Prior to the recession, the Organization for International Investment analyzed greenfield, or entirely new projects, and found they have been creating between 30,000 and 55,000 new jobs annually in the United States since 2006.[5] Overall employment by foreign companies in the United States grew from 5.1 million in 2006 to 5.3 million in 2008, a net increase of nearly 200,000. It then jumped to 5.5 million in 2009, an increase of roughly 200,000 in just one year. This latter big jump, despite the Great Recession, may well have been caused by factors such as a rising Euro that has subsequently dropped sharply due to the Greek debt crisis and could be an anomaly.

For our framework, the benefit of jobs insourced to the United States will be estimated as roughly 100,000 new jobs created annually from the combination of both new, greenfield projects as well as organic growth at existing operations, notwithstanding any major shifts due to the current economic crisis.

CHAPTER 14

Innovation Companies

A COMMON QUESTION is whether or not companies that use outsourcing can also create high-value jobs in America. The answer has to do with the evolution of a breed of company that outsources its manufacturing in order to focus on the higher value activities of product design, marketing, and distribution.

Why this trend benefits American companies and creates high-value jobs in America is illustrated by the "smiley curve" described by James Fallows in an article in *The Atlantic*. The smiley curve is the U shape showing the profitability of the stages in a typical product life cycle. It's very high at either end—with product design, branding, and marketing on the left and retail sales on the right being the two most profitable activities. In the middle is the manufacturing step, the bottom part of the U-shaped curve which is the least profitable activity of all.

Fallows cites several examples: an Ethernet cable made in China sells in the United States for $19.95, but only $2 of the value stays in China. A $30 audio device manufactured in China leaves just $6 of the value in China—the other $24 is captured by the companies developing the product and the ones retailing it.[6]

Consider Apple as a real world example of the Smiley curve in action. Apple's iPod has been phenomenally successful. Between its launch in 2000 and the latest sales numbers in 2009, Apple sold 218 million iPods and earned $38 billion.[7] That's from just one product in Apple's ecosystem of products. The iPhone has challenged competitors like Nokia and Motorola for domination of the smartphone market. More recently Apple launched the iPad, a tablet media device, which sold 3 million copies—each at least $499— in just the first 80 days after it was launched in 2010. It has subsequently sold tens of millions of iPads and defined an entire category. In fact, Apple has been so enormously successful as a company with its popular products that in May 2010 it overtook Microsoft to become the world's most valuable technology company with a total stock value of $227 billion.[8]

Yet the entire manufacturing effort for Apple's enormously popular products from iPods to iPads is completely outsourced. Instead of manufacturing, Apple focuses on what it does best: designing and engineering breakthrough products and then marketing those products with hip media campaigns and selling them through cool retail outlets.

So what does that mean for American workers? In a draft working paper, Greg Linden, Kenneth Kraemer, and Jason Dedrick of the Sloan Foundation's Personal Computing Industry Center estimated the job and salary impacts of the iPod across its global supply chain. In 2006, they estimated there were 41,170 jobs associated with producing the iPod. Of these, just shy of 14,000 were in the United States. The rest were primarily in Asia Pacific among suppliers of components for the iPod. Japan produced some of the key, specialized electronic components. Final assembly was done in China. China accounted for some 12,270 jobs, over 90 percent of which were in manufacturing assembly.

The total wages paid to employees in the United States working on the iPod (from engineering to retail) was $745 million. The total wages paid overseas was less than half that at $318.5 million. Japanese workers accounted for $102 million of that total. Several other suppliers around Asia earned a share. Chinese workers earned just $23.5 million for the low-cost, manual labor that goes into assembling the iPod.[9]

Apple's iPod illustrates the benefits of outsourcing and how American workers gain high-paying jobs and an oversized share of the total wages when companies specialize in product design, engineering, marketing, and distribution. The paper confirms what James Fallows had written in *The Atlantic*. The real money is not in manufacturing, and Americans gain the lion's share of the benefits of outsourcing by designing and then selling the product themselves while outsourcing production.

Using outsourcing, a company can rapidly scale up a new product and create a breakthrough winner. They can challenge incumbents (some of which might be foreign producers) and create entirely new product categories, resulting in new jobs in America. Without outsourcing, companies would have to build their own factories at enormous expense, and many products like the iPod, iPhone, and iPad would never reach the market because they would be too expensive to produce, or they would launch at a price point that is too high for too long, meaning much lower sales. Without outsourcing, Apple would likely be a fraction of its size today and most of us might never have had a chance to buy an iPhone or iPad.

Apple's story is not unique. Vizio is another American company that has used outsourcing to quickly enter a market, scale production (in this case of digital TVs) and, in the space of a few years, challenge industry incumbents—Sony and Samsung—for leadership. In 2005, Vizio sold just over $140 million in TVs. By the end of 2007, revenue was nearing $2 billion, a stunning accomplishment directly resulting from the ability to scale production (through outsourcing) very quickly.[10] In 2010, Vizio hit $2 billion and beat Sony on total sales. Now they are closing in on Samsung.[11]

This is not a new phenomenon. Nike started its business a generation ago with exactly the same model—outsourcing the manufacturing (originally to Japanese companies that were then the low-cost manufacturers in shoes) while focusing on product design and distribution at home. By 2009, it had become a company with 34,000 employees around the world (not including contract manufacturers), with annual revenue of $19.2 billion, and ranking in the Fortune 500.[12]

Apple is killing Nokia in smartphones. Vizio is beating Sony in TVs. Both are examples of fast-moving companies that quickly innovate and use outsourcing to manufacture, and they aren't alone.

Outsourcing offers American entrepreneurs and companies the ability to focus on innovation by outsourcing the least profitable portion of the value chain—manufacturing. The result is that American companies and workers frequently capture the majority of the total product value, earn higher wages, and pay more taxes at home, supporting America's public services.

Unfortunately, a definitive number of net new jobs created in the United States by such firms is not available. Apple, Vizio, and Nike are not alone, but I have not seen any specific data quantifying how many firms and how many new jobs are being created within the American economy by firms that fit this profile. For now, our framework can only acknowledge that these companies exist, but cannot offer a total number of jobs created annually in America from them.

Chapter 15

Profits

OUTSOURCING ALLOWS companies to cut costs and increase profits. This much is clear. But is there any kind of moral or social benefit from bigger profits?

If these cost-cutting moves and stock-price jumps are purely for the self-aggrandizement of CEOs and do not help the company prosper over the long term, then the pundits are right and this is both ethically wrong and unsustainable for the companies themselves.

However, there are two possible benefits from increasing profitability that are often ignored when the popular outrage over CEO pay is being stoked. These need to be explicitly articulated as moral and social benefits so that we understand why profits, and actions that increase them, are important both socially and economically.

The first benefit to consider is the role of profits in the ability to invest in the future. If a company has strong cash flow, it can afford to invest in innovative new products and services that will result in future earnings. (That doesn't mean they will, it just means they can—an important distinction.) New investments tend to create jobs in product development, design, research, and IT. These are generally high-paying jobs. They are often in the core areas of what companies consider proprietary, so they are less willing to move them offshore. If the company is located in the United States, then a good share of these jobs are likely to be created in the United States.

Not all companies are so successful. Many make the wrong bets or follow the wrong strategy. For every market leader there is a crowded pack of followers fighting to survive and find their niche. Many of these companies are under enormous pressure. They don't have the best products and can't charge premium prices. Some of these companies will face dire financial challenges and fail.

When companies are on the ropes financially, they effectively consume their nest egg. Thus, profitability is directly connected to the ability to innovate and create products and services that drive future profits and jobs. Outsourcing, to the extent that it helps in this process (by lowering costs and diverting cash to innovation activities), creates a tangible benefit that should not be dismissed.

This sounds like the business case, but from a political and economic perspective, we *want* companies to be profitable and to be creating high-paying jobs at home. Outsourcing is one of the mechanisms by which they can do this.

There is another benefit to profitability. Nearly half of all Americans own stock or bonds. According to the Investment Company Institute and the Securities Industry Association's "Equity Ownership in America" 2008 report, around 47 percent of all American households own stock.[13] The vast majority of stock owners—88 percent—are investing in stocks to save for retirement, often through defined contribution plans and their 401k.[14] More than 45 percent of American retirees' income comes from private savings such as 401k and stocks.[15] For a broad swath of Americans, financial security in retirement depends on private savings in the form of stock ownership and the performance and success of the companies whose stock they own. There is a social benefit in having profitable companies with high stock prices, and outsourcing helps those companies be successful and build higher stock prices.

The baby boomers are seeing this firsthand. The recent economic crisis and resulting fall in stock prices undermined the Boomers' stock portfolios (although some of this has recovered). Due to their age, Boomers have less time to make up for any losses to their investments, and the economic crisis occurred at the very moment when they should have been shifting out of volatile stocks to more stable, but lower-earning investments such as bonds and money market funds.

For many Boomers, the implication is either a deferred retirement or a reduced lifestyle. Just 13 percent of American workers now say they are very confident in having enough money to live comfortably in retirement, down sharply over the last two years. Approximately 72 percent of American workers expect to continue working after they retire.[16] This represents a looming crisis on the horizon. For Boomers, improving stock prices—by increasing the prospects for growth and profitability—is an urgent necessity.

There is a widespread social benefit when companies are profitable. Outsourcing contributes to this picture as one tool that companies have to decrease costs and boost innovation to drive future revenues. As companies prosper and their stock prices go up, it helps increase the financial assets that almost half of all Americans are relying on to finance their future retirement.

CHAPTER 16

Saving Jobs

OUTSOURCING IS WIDELY reviled as a cause of job loss. But by allowing companies to preserve businesses that would otherwise fail—to reduce costs and remain viable in the face of competitive threats—it also results in companies surviving and, therefore, jobs being saved.

One of the best—and most ironic—examples of how outsourcing can save a company is Stanley Tools, described in Louis Uchitelle's book *The Disposable American*. Uchitelle budgets plenty of time to criticize the offshoring of jobs at Stanley. Yet he also articulates the business challenge Stanley Tools faced at the time, namely Asian competitors bringing similar products into the market at prices 60 percent lower and customers switching to these competitors in large numbers.[17]

For any company, this threat could lead to business failure, a shutdown, or downsizing that would see jobs lost in vast numbers. After all, even the most powerful multinational corporation cannot compel people to buy its products at prices vastly higher than competitors'. How long could Stanley have lasted if it continued losing market share? If it failed, how many workers would have been out of jobs?

Stanley survived by moving production offshore. American jobs were lost in the process. This is clear, and Uchitelle rebukes the executives for their callous disregard for these self-same American jobs. But the company survived and continues to do so today. In the process, some American jobs were also saved. How many jobs were saved—and which ones—is not made clear.

Should the measure of success be how many jobs are lost or how many are saved? Not every decision to outsource is in the face of a competitive threat or a crisis-inspired struggle to survive. In fact, well-managed firms avoid these crises by constantly seeking avenues to reduce costs and maintain operational discipline and efficiency. Like athletes in constant training, successful companies must continually work to maintain their muscle tone of operational efficiency.

A more apt analogy might be a treadmill. The life of a business is a constantly moving treadmill. Forward progress is made with innovation, new products, and cost cutting, and productivity gains. Stop any of these activities and the business stops moving—and it is on its way to falling off the treadmill into the zone of business failure.

Offshore outsourcing is one business tool that can help companies survive. It results in lost jobs, but jobs are also preserved. The benefits in this context are not as visible as the negative headlines on layoffs, and I know no way of quantifying them, but they are real nonetheless.

CHAPTER 17

Trade-Related Jobs

OUTSOURCING DIRECTLY and indirectly creates American jobs ranging from the export and import sectors to resource jobs. I'll provide a couple of snapshots below to illustrate this point.

Export Jobs

Outsourcing plays a role in catalyzing economic growth in developing countries. This growth feeds back as a benefit to America in the form of increased export opportunities and the jobs these exports create.

If anyone doubts the potential value of exports to markets like China and India now and in the future, I have just one word for them—nuts. By which, of course, I mean almonds, pecans, and walnuts. China was on track to becoming the largest buyer of American almonds in 2010. In 2009 China was the top destination for American pecans. In 2007 it was the biggest foreign market for walnuts. In just five years, export sales to China of US tree nuts grew from $89 million to $737 million. This growth has been explosive by any measure.

It happened because the American nut industry actively marketed to and created demand within China's increasingly large consumer market. But this surprising success story illustrates the growing potential of Chinese (and other developing countries') demand and how it might begin to impact American exports as well as jobs in the United States.[18]

How does this dimension of job creation measure up?

In 2000 US exports totaled just $1 trillion. By 2008 they had reached $1.86 trillion, an increase of 86 percent. In 2000 exports to China alone were only $16.1 billion. By 2008 they had increased to $69.7 billion.[19]

The question then is how much credit can outsourcing claim, either directly or indirectly for this success and the associated jobs?

Outsourcing has driven a big portion of China's export economy, which is in turn roughly 45 percent of its overall economy. The foreign investment into China and the foreign exchange earned from exports has catalyzed rapid growth throughout the Chinese domestic economy. This economic growth has resulted in jobs and income and, in aggregate, the growth of a new consumer market. Thus, there is a pretty good case that American exports to China are indirectly, but solidly, related to outsourcing.

China is not the only country we outsource to. American companies also outsource significant production to Mexico, Canada, Brazil, India, and Costa Rica to name just a few. All of these countries are also ones we export to.

This is today, but the real prize is the future. China—despite the hype surroundings its growth—remains predominantly a poor country. So does India. But that picture is beginning to change. The reality is beginning to catch up with the hype.

One study by the McKinsey Global Institute found that China's total consumer economy is already the size of Italy's. The problem is that China's average spending is just $543 per person per year (although the average hides wide inequalities). Yet McKinsey believes that Chinese incomes are increasing rapidly and predicts that a massive middle class will emerge over the next ten years. China may become the third largest consumer market by 2025, and the disposable income of China's new middle class could reach $2.7 trillion, of which the top part of the middle class (the part most able to spend) will have 61 percent.[20]

Those middle class incomes in absolute dollar terms will be relatively small at $3,000 to $12,000. But McKinsey notes that the purchasing power parity of that income will be the equivalent of $13,000 to $54,000 in US dollars. Purchasing power parity is important. If people are spending much less on housing and food in dollar terms, they have significant spending power to purchase consumer goods, like tree nuts, and services.

McKinsey isn't alone in seeing this trend. A study by the World Bank also highlights the rise of a new global middle class in the developing world. If pre-crisis growth projections hold up over the long run, by the year 2030, the global middle class could reach nearly 1.2 billion people, from just 400 million today.[21]

The World Bank isn't just talking about China. India has been experiencing rapid economic growth and is developing a consumer market of its own. In 2005 the Indian middle class was still relatively small at 5 percent of the population (13 million households, or 50 million people). However, by 2025 India's market will be the fifth largest in the world, surpassing the size of Germany's consumer market.[22] It may also be a much bigger destination for American exports at that point.

Outsourcing has a role in catalyzing growth overseas in markets ranging from China to India, and Brazil to Eastern Europe. These markets already purchase US exports now and will do so more in the future, creating growth and jobs in the US economy as a result.

John Watkins of the American Chamber of Commerce in China was quoted as saying that "Three One Trillions" is possible in US–China business relations over the next thirty years. He meant that US companies will export $1 trillion to China, US companies operating in China will hit $1 trillion in annual revenues for the Chinese domestic market, and Chinese companies will invest a cumulative $1 trillion in foreign direct investment in the United States.[23] These are big numbers and seem well within the realm of possibility given a thirty-year time span. They are also for just one market: China.

The seemingly inescapable conclusion is that the global economic pie is getting bigger, and America has a chance to grow and export more because of it—creating more American jobs in the process.

Mining Jobs

Mining is another example of positive feedback caused by higher prices driven by increased demand. As recently as 2003, the US Bureau of Labor Statistics was forecasting mining employment in the United States to decrease by nearly 9 percent, or some 46,000 jobs, by 2014. Total employment in the mining sector had declined from 771,000 in 1987 to just 572,000 in 2003.[24] The forecast predicted technology gains, worker productivity, increased competition, and stricter regulations would all combine to drive employment lower in the mining sector.

Then something surprising happened. Around 2003—shortly after the bureau made its forecast—mining employment turned on a dime and started growing rapidly, increasing nearly 20 percent in just three years.

By 2006, mining employment had jumped to 684,000, an increase of over 100,000 jobs and the highest levels seen since the early 1990s.[25]

The mining industry had entered an upturn driven by higher prices and increased demand, what many called a super-cycle. Mining jobs pay well—an average of $56,000 per year (at a time when median household income in the United States is just a bit over $50,000 per year)—and the industry itself says it will need at least another 55,000 workers over the next five to ten years to replace retiring workers and to meet continued demand.[26]

What happened? Economic growth in China—sparked in part by the growth of outsourcing—dramatically increased the demand for all mineral resources needed to build infrastructure, cities, and industry. While the global economic crisis temporarily dented demand for many of these commodities, high prices have quickly returned as demand, especially in China, has picked up.

As China's economy and impact on global trade continues to grow, new demand is being created throughout the mining sector. In 2010 the United States began to export large amounts of coal to China— nearly 3 million tons in the first six months.[27] Disputes over rare earth mining, almost wholly supplied by China today, now means that mining operations previously closed in the United States due to lack of need will almost certainly begin again.

China will eventually slow down, but it is not the only large and rapidly growing emerging market. India, Brazil, Indonesia, and others are on the same track. As they grow, they too will need to build everything from infrastructure to urban housing. The super-cycle of metal and mineral demand looks set to continue. This higher level of demand around the world and the higher prices they create will help drive more jobs and higher incomes in the United States in the coming years.

Import Jobs

The United States imported $2.1 trillion in merchandise in 2008 and $1.95 billion in 2009. There are many jobs associated with these imports: the workers who unload the ships, the truck drivers and train engineers who move the goods across the United States, the workers in distribution centers that remix the incoming shipments into outbound deliveries. Then, too, there are the store employees who unload the products as well as all of the retail workers associated with selling the goods. Let's not forget the managerial, legal, and business professional jobs associated with all of the companies engaged in importing. The vast distribution and sales systems associated with moving outsourced goods into the United States and selling them to consumers supports literally millions of jobs.

Consider ports. Trade—driven in large part by outsourcing production and creating global supply chains—increased container volume by 41 percent between 2002 and 2006 from 11 million units to nearly 16 million. One result was an increase in longshoreman jobs represented by the International Longshore and Werehouse Union, growing nearly 38 percent from 10,283 in 2002 to nearly 14,000 in 2006. These jobs pay an average of $127,000 before overtime.[28]

The economic crisis put the brakes on some of this growth, but as growth returns, so will this storyline. Not too long ago, industry officials were calling for a big increase in infrastructure to allow for greater traffic.[29] Once the American economy starts to pick up steam, infrastructure job creation in this area will surge as well.

Once moribund, American railways have become growth stocks for investors and sources of jobs for American workers. In fact, the industry will need to invest heavily in new lines, cars, engines, and employees to meet growing demand for rail which is cheaper and more energy efficient than trucking goods across the country.[30] This will, in turn, create yet more jobs in America.

Summary

Trade-related activities, imports and exports, accounted for approximately 38.4 million US jobs in 2008, according to an analysis done for the Business Roundtable.[31] This has grown from 31 million jobs in 2004, a rate of gain of over 1.8 million jobs per year. By 2008, over one in five US jobs were related to trade.

Outsourcing's overall role in this is hard to pin down, but a good proxy is China-related trade given the heavy influence outsourcing as an industry has had on China's economy. Between 2004 and 2008, imports and exports between China and the United States grew from $231 billion to $407 billion. China's share of total US trade grew from roughly 7.75 percent to 9.3 percent.

Job creation directly and indirectly related to outsourcing in the trade-related sector can be estimated at approximately 300,000 new jobs per year between 2004 and 2008. China, as noted earlier, is not the only country that we outsource to that may be directly and indirectly creating jobs in the United States. However, to be conservative, we will use China as a proxy for total jobs in the trade-related sector (imports and exports) created or influenced by outsourcing.

CHAPTER 18

Outsourcing Unemployment

THERE IS A POTENTIAL benefit to outsourcing that has to date received little attention. I believe that the aggregate impact of outsourcing *may* serve to reduce the vulnerability of the US economy to mass unemployment from economic shocks, creating significant social and political benefits both now and in the future.

This is counterintuitive. Most people see offshore outsourcing as causing job loss and creating higher unemployment. This is partly true. However, outsourcing is a gradual process that impacts, as we have seen, around 2 percent of the total jobs lost in any given year across the economy. In terms of mechanisms that reallocate workers within the economy, this one is relatively small, but potentially quite important. This is because the types of jobs that are lost are primarily (albeit not wholly) those in labor-intensive manufacturing and simple, repetitive IT and business processing.

Given this dynamic, there are two cases in which outsourcing may help avoid massive unemployment shocks and help us to recover faster from those that we experience. The first is an economic crisis—exactly like the one whose aftershocks we are living through right now. The second is in the event of a transition to automated production driven by leaps in technology such as artificial intelligence.

Let's start with the crisis scenario. We recently experienced a global economic crisis that most now agree was the biggest since the Great Depression of the 1930s. Many of the indicators tracked the 1930s experience. For example, the drop-off in world trade during the early phases of this crisis was on par with that experienced during the Great Depression.[32] We could even see a double dip just as they did in the Great Depression.

Unemployment is a major factor after the recent crisis, and in 2011 it was slowly ticking down from its high above 10 percent. However, broader measures of unemployment that include people who have dropped out of the workforce as well as people who are underemployed (e.g., couldn't find a full-time job) remain stubbornly high and in the range of 15 to 17 percent.[33]

In round numbers this is an appalling 25 to 26 million Americans who are either unemployed (14.5 million), underemployed (8.6 million), or have given up looking for work entirely (1 to 2 million). Yet as bad as this is, it is still nowhere close to the nearly 25 percent unemployment experienced in the Great Depression. The difference is an additional 10 to 15 million Americans that would be unemployed today.

Why this difference? Government stimulus efforts may deserve part of the credit for maintaining sufficient demand to avoid larger job losses, although there is some controversy over how much. While there is extensive debate about how many jobs the US stimulus created, it did preserve many public sector jobs. And the public sector is much bigger than it was in the 1930s. There are likely many factors.

But outsourcing may also have made a difference in lowering the structural vulnerability to higher unemployment levels. As demand for goods dropped off in late 2008 and early 2009 as a result of the crisis, China witnessed a vast drop-off in exports and a reported loss of over 20 million factory jobs by migrant workers. At the same time, the United States also experienced a big drop in manufacturing employment.

But what if those manufacturing jobs now in China had remained in the United States when this crisis had struck? The factory closures and job losses in the United States would have been broader, deeper, and more severe than seen to date. Many more American workers would be out of jobs. The small businesses with workers that indirectly rely on these jobs would also have scaled back even further than they have in this crisis, amplifying the impact. The total unemployment rate would be higher—potentially even approaching Great Depression–era levels.

What outsourcing may have done in shifting work abroad during the years before the recession is transfer the unemployment associated with losing that work when demand dropped. Outsourcing may have also reduced the stimulus costs required for us to support those extra millions of workers in their search for new jobs. Finally, and perhaps most importantly, we may have limited the potential damage to market psychology and public confidence that much higher levels of unemployment would have created. That, in turn, may mean that outsourcing helped our economy avoid a period of greater consumer retrenchment and a deeper, more prolonged crisis.

I've focused on manufacturing, but something similar may be beginning to take shape in services. In March 2011, AOL purchased the *Huffington Post* and promptly announced it was cutting 900 people as it consolidated and prepared to integrate the new company. But there was something unique about this particular set of redundancies. Just 200 of these lost jobs were in America; the other 700 were in India.[34]

The AOL announcement may have presaged a new balance in how job losses occur in the future. Many US multinational companies have spent a decade reorganizing their operations and now include global workforces instead of the predominantly American ones of ten to fifteen years ago. As corporations reorganize and acquire other companies, future job loss in functions, such as IT, and business processes, such as finance and accounting, may fall less and less on Americans and more on foreign workers. AOL's actions may be an indicator of future business decisions in the event of another sudden economic downturn.

My speculation about the future balance of job loss is theoretical and unproven, but it is a potential benefit worth considering and studying.

There is another potential benefit on the horizon from outsourcing. As technology advances, artificial intelligence and robotics have the potential to take on many more jobs than they do now. Progress in artificial intelligence, speech recognition, and computing power will likely result in millions of lower-skill jobs—everything from call center work to medical transcription—being automated away.[35]

In February 2011, IBM's Watson computer successfully beat humans at the game of Jeopardy. This triumph for artificial intelligence may well represent a seminal event with far-reaching impacts. In the field of robotics, research is underway on such delicate tasks as tending tomato plants.[36] If a robot can be developed to pluck a tomato, how long before it can accurately assemble an iPod or an iPhone? With the rapid pace of progress, many commentators have expressed concern at the potential impact on employment in the United States.[37]

In such a scenario, it is important to point out that the jobs—at least initially—that are the most vulnerable from automation and productivity gains are the ones that are simple and repetitive. A significant portion of such jobs have already been outsourced overseas. Outsourcing is helping to steadily transform the US economy, and by doing so, it may—in some small way—also be helping to reduce the vulnerability of US workers to larger unemployment shocks in the future.

The idea that outsourcing may be helping us—now and in the future—avoid larger unemployment shocks is theoretical. It is worth considering, but it can't be reliably quantified.

CHAPTER 19

Migrant Opportunity

I COVERED LABOR exploitation in the Costs section, but there is another dimension to the dynamic of migrant labor which is directly and indirectly driven by the outsourcing industry: the opportunity it provides migrants—especially young women—to improve their lives and escape the shackles of rural village life.

My starting point for this perspective is an African village. As a Peace Corps volunteer, I lived for two years in a small, rural African farming village complete with grass roof huts. Here is my take on the subject of migrant opportunity: village life in a developing country is only idyllic and romantic to casual tourists and their fleeting impressions. For the people who live their lives in rural villages, life is hard, short, and bereft of many of the things we developed-country urbanites take for granted, from health care to entertainment. Village life is at times crushingly boring. At other times—like before the harvest when last year's food has run out—it is deeply anxiety ridden and accompanied by malnourishment.

It is not a safe place to live. People sicken or die from causes as varied as infections in the cuts and wounds of daily farm work, mosquito bites swelling with disease, wasting lung diseases from the soot and smoke off the cooking fires, snake bites received while walking along a trail to the fields, or waterborne diseases from lack of sewage and water treatment facilities. The work day begins at or before dawn and runs into the night, especially for women, whose labor is constant. Living conditions are crowded. Whole families often sleep in one tiny room of a mud-brick hut with a thatch roof—itself a home to rodents and reptiles. Kids get the floor and a sleeping mat in the corner, or they go outside if the weather is warm.

Life in a village means everyone knows your business—and involves themselves in it. Village life is stifling for the young. During my time in a village, I realized how many of the young people desperately wanted to move to the big city. Many tried, but in Africa it is harder to do. There are few jobs and fewer factories. If you go down country to stay with relatives and can't earn your keep, then you can't remain without being a burden. They can't afford to host you. So back you come.

For women, village life is doubly hard. Social roles are traditional. In the village I lived in, I attended several village councils. These were affairs run exclusively by men. I don't recall seeing a woman in the role of village chief or women attending village councils except to provide testimony where decisions were made about and for them. Women raised the kids and tended the fields and cooked the food. They didn't necessarily get an equal say in decisions.

My experience in an African village may seem distant from countries such as China and India impacted by outsourcing, but it is closer than some might think. In *Last Train Home*, a 2009 documentary film by Lixin Fan, the story of a migrant family in China illustrates the breakdown of the traditional rural family. A married couple, Changhua and Suqin, have spent seventeen years working in the factories of Guangzhou, leaving their two children to be raised by their grandmother back in the village. Changua and Suqin are able to return home just once a year. At the reunion featured in the movie, they barely recognize their oldest child, Qin, a seventeen-year old girl who is angry that they abandoned her. While the parents watch in dismay, Qin drops out of school against her parents' wishes and migrates to Guangzhou to find work.[38]

The story of one family torn apart and the agonizing choice the parents have made to work far from home and miss out on raising their own children is painful to watch. Yet it is a story played out across China on a scale of tens of millions as parents in rural areas leave children behind to move to coastal cities for jobs in factories, construction, or services. The Chinese government estimates there are 58 million left-behind children—20 percent of all children in China and nearly 50 percent of all children in the countryside.[39]

The breakdown of family relationships and traditional rural village life doesn't sound like a positive point, but look a little closer and there is another reality that starts to peek through. Village life for Qin is boring and seems to promise no future. Her move to the city follows a well-trodden path paved not only by her parents but also by most of the other young people in her village seeking opportunity. Once she arrives in the city, the film captures hard work, poor living conditions, and dubious prospects for the future. But it also portrays fleeting glimpses of independence and freedom: Qin having drinks and eating dinner with her friends, getting her hair done in a salon downtown, going to the mall to buy clothes. All of it unsupervised in the anonymity of the city where what she chooses to do is no one's business but her own.

These are activities that many people in developed countries take for granted (including documentary filmmakers and activists), but for millions upon millions of people in poor, developing countries, life in the big city is a chance for adventure and opportunity. It's a chance to escape the boredom of the rural village and experience the world. It's a shot at freedom from parents, village gossip, and a fate set in stone.

The film provides just brief glimpses, but this reality of girls migrating to the city for jobs, freedom, and opportunity is the whole subject of Leslie Chang's book *Factory Girls*. In it, Chang spends time getting to know the young girls working in the factories of southeastern China, and she sees these girls less as victims than as strong-willed, brave, and adventurous people. She describes the migrants that choose to go out, our *chuqu*, as the "rural elite," and they make this leap to the cities not just for money but for a chance to change their fate, improve themselves, and see the world beyond the rural village.[40]

For young women in particular, migrating to the city to work in a factory gives them unprecedented freedom from parental authority and influence. Chang profiles a young woman named Min who sends money home and gains an enormous amount of leverage in the relationship with her parents to the point of influencing how they spend the money she has sent them. Money is power, and soon Min is also counseling her younger brothers and sisters.[41]

The girls that stay in the village are stuck with their fate. Village life is stultifying and rigid. Roles are set for life. In most developing countries, it confers a life of poverty and subjugation to the will of male elders.

What's true in Africa and China is also true in India. A 2011 article in the *New York Times* profiled the *khap panchayats*, or village councils of unelected male elders, in rural India and how they exert influence on the communities they preside over, to the point of superseding national law. These khap panchayats have a role in supporting social cohesion and traditional norms as well as of mediating conflicts, which are all good things. But they have also been implicated in the honor killings of young women who marry or engage in relationships without approval. These village councils are male-dominated and play a primary role in enforcing rigid social norms from which many young people cannot escape.[42]

Migration is a chance to abandon these stifling and unfair councils and start over. It is not easy (as the chapter on labor exploitation discussed), but there is a reason that people make this choice. It goes far beyond simply a pursuit for money. People want an opportunity for a better life. In places like China, where rural villagers have a chance to decide for themselves what is best, tens of millions have voted with their feet to leave rural life.

Outsourcing as an industry is directly responsible in large part for creating such opportunities. It does not do so with any form of altruistic intent, of course. But the practical reality is that migrants on a massive scale in China, India, and many other countries get a chance to create a new future with opportunities that are rarely available in the small, rural villages that they come from, and this advantage needs to be considered as a benefit of outsourcing.

CHAPTER 20

Poverty Reduction

IF THERE IS ANYTHING we can agree on across all political boundaries, it is that poverty is bad and should be eliminated. A study funded by the German Marshall Fund of the United States found that large majorities in both the United States (72 percent) and Europe (75 percent) favor providing aid to poor countries to alleviate poverty. Many European countries are even stronger in their support than the United States (Italy: 94 percent, France: 83 percent, UK: 77 percent).[43]

And yet the harsh reality is that poverty remains endemic to the human species. Consider the following facts about our world of 7 billion people:

- 1.4 billion live on less than $1.25/day—below which is considered "extreme poverty," according to the World Bank
- 9 million children under five years old die from preventable illnesses each year in poor countries
- 884 million people in developing countries lack access to clean drinking water
- 2.5 billion people lack access to basic sanitation such as toilets.[44]

Such numbers are shocking, and yet they barely speak to the colossal loss of talent, creativity, and output of people who never reach their potential because the basics of education, health, and security are missing for such a large portion of humanity. How many potential Einsteins, da Vincis, Beethovens, or even Buffetts fail to overcome the poverty of their surroundings? What could humanity be capable of if all its members had an equal chance at the start?

Against this backdrop of appalling poverty, we are witnessing one of the most profound transformations in human history—a massive, unprecedented reduction in global poverty through economic growth. The number of people living in extreme poverty in China alone has dropped by 475 million over the last twenty years.[45] "The Millennium Development Goals Report 2010" documents the speed with which this picture is changing. The percentage of the population in East Asia living on less than $1.25 per day fell from 60 percent in 1990 to 16 percent in 2005, beating even the MGD's goal of a 50 percent reduction by 2015 by fully a decade. China is on track to decrease this rate to below 5 percent by 2015, just a few years from now.[46]

These changes are nothing less than astounding. They are the result of a massive wave of employment that almost directly tracks the role of outsourcing in moving production to China. Indirectly, outsourcing has catalyzed a large employment boom in infrastructure construction (railroads, ports, real estate) to sustain the migration of rural job seekers to the more prosperous, faster-growing urban centers along China's eastern seaboard. The economic progress in China has very little to do with aid and everything to do with jobs on a massive scale.

While a decade or so behind China, India is also benefiting from a boom in outsourcing, which now accounts for nearly $50 billion in revenue per year.[47] While this revenue is small in comparison to China's massive export earnings, it is enough to have begun catalyzing profound changes in India's domestic economy. Nasscom estimates that the industry directly supports 2 million employees and indirectly another 8 million. However, this probably understates the numbers since each job holder also supports a household and, often, an extended family. Ultimately, the number of people supported by the outsourcing industry in India may be far higher.

Indian industry and government are also preparing to invest massively in the infrastructure, from roads and railways to ports and cities, needed to continue economic growth.[48] And while India has largely captured outsourcing in service industries, over the coming decade, the country is poised to capture a share of electronics manufacturing outsourcing as well, perhaps at China's expense.[49]

From these examples, it should be obvious. Outsourcing as an industry is driving job creation and its associated multiplier effect in developing countries. It is unromantic, basely motivated by self-interest and profit, and also exceptionally effective.

Poverty reduction, then, is a moral benefit of outsourcing. Jobs are created in China and India (and other countries). A multiplier effect creates additional employment throughout the domestic economy in the form of construction, services, and supporting jobs. A middle class is slowly built. Extreme poverty is reduced as jobs in everything from construction to service industries are created and filled by the unskilled poor. Global poverty reduction on a massive scale is one benefit of outsourcing, lifting nearly 500 million people out of extreme poverty in China alone.

CONCLUSION

Conventional wisdom declares that corporate America is selling out this country by moving jobs overseas. In fact, the picture is more complex and there are a number of benefits that Americans gain from outsourcing and offshoring.

Part II of this book has created a partial list—a framework, if you will—for discussing and weighing offshore outsourcing's benefits to both America and the world. The benefits identified include the following:

Cheaper Goods: Americans save an estimated $1,000 per individual or $2,500 per household due to cheaper products available through outsourcing. This number may be conservative given that the benefit to the economy as a whole of global trade has been estimated at $1 trillion.

Better Service: Americans benefit from greatly enhanced customer service and support from outsourcing. The concept of ubiquitous 24-7 support would have seemed astonishing a generation ago. Across many industries it is now a basic requirement.

Insourcing: There are 5.35 million jobs that have been created by foreign companies insourcing jobs to America. The rate of growth is estimated at around 100,000 new jobs each year from greenfield projects and organic growth. (In 2009, the number was closer to 200,000, but this might have been an anomaly.)

Innovation Focus: Companies such as Apple, Vizio, and Nike show how companies that outsource manufacturing and focus domestic talent on product design and distribution can create many high-paying jobs in America and capture a large share of the value chain in producing the goods. Total jobs created are likely contained within the trade-related job category below.

Profits: Now more than ever, American workers are relying on private savings, most often in the form of stock ownership, to provide them a comfortable living in retirement. Companies that can generate healthy profits and sustained growth are critical for the baby boomers to have enough money in retirement.

Saving Jobs: While it cannot be quantified, outsourcing helps companies save jobs by cutting costs and remaining more competitive in the face of tough market conditions.

Trade-Related Jobs: Jobs are created directly and indirectly within the US economy from the growth of trade through both exports and imports. Parsing out those specific to outsourcing, a subset of overall trade, is challenging, but a rough estimate using China as a proxy suggests that the United States gained a minimum of 300,000 jobs per year between 2004 and 2008. This might be conservative. According to a Business Roundtable analysis, total trade-related job growth in those same years was running at around 1.8 million additional jobs per year.

Outsourcing Unemployment: A radical premise has also been offered to suggest that outsourcing has provided a social and political benefit to America by reducing the amplitude of shocks from unemployment in a major economic crisis or a revolutionary leap in technology-driven productivity gains.

Migrant Opportunity: Migration is a chance for individuals to overturn fate and start over, avoiding the rigid social roles of rural village life. Outsourcing has created this opportunity on a massive scale for people—especially young women—in places like China and India to create a better future for themselves.

Poverty Reduction: Outsourcing is a huge part of China's growth story, and this economic growth has resulted in East Asia reducing the incidence of extreme poverty by nearly 500 million people and beating the United Nations' Millennium Development Goal for the region fully ten years early. Outsourcing is a major contributor to poverty reduction in developing countries.

Summary

Overall, the list above documents a broad set of benefits to outsourcing both for America and the world. It is not meant to be comprehensive or complete, but illustrative. It's a starting point, not an end point.

In some cases, I have quantified the benefits based on the information I have. In other areas, I have not found data to provide a quantitative estimate. In both cases, I invite readers to share their insights, perspectives, and estimates by joining the debate on *www.themoralcase.com*.

The important point is that we now have a framework in place on both sides of the ledger. With that framework, it is possible to assess the moral case on outsourcing and to determine how the costs and benefits weigh up for both America and the world.

PART 3
THE MORAL CASE

OVERVIEW

"BE THE TABLE!"

I sat wide-eyed as the professor, a disheveled fellow, draped himself over a table and emphatically uttered those words.

The memory comes back easily. I was a young college student, and I had impulsively signed up for a 400-level course in Existential Philosophy—without the benefit of any prior training or prerequisites. And here was the professor, at the very start of one of the first classes, illustrating a point from one of our texts on Kierkegaard, Sartre, or one of the others. I was hopelessly lost and painfully aware of it. I didn't even have the goatee that most of my classmates were sporting. I dropped the class and counted myself lucky to have escaped.

It was a simple lesson still relevant today. I am not and cannot pretend to be a professional philosopher or a moral ethicist. (I still don't have a goatee.) What I can do is take these next steps in weighing the moral case on outsourcing with caution, good faith, and my best efforts to be as fair as possible.

Our exploration of the moral case began with some profound questions about the nature of outsourcing, how it fits into the global economy, and how good or bad it is for America and the world. These are big questions. To address them, I presented a broad array of facts on both sides of the debate in the form of the costs and benefits in the preceding sections and chapters. Now, it is time to determine where on the spectrum the moral position of outsourcing really lies: good, bad, or ugly.

Before beginning, there are additional factors to consider. There is the issue of confirmation bias, discussed earlier. How do I avoid unintentional bias and earn your trust as a reader when of course I also want to come out looking like the good guy in the end? The answer is brutally simple: I am biased. I cannot pretend to be otherwise.

Having owned up to the obvious, is there a way to overcome the bias? I believe this is possible by creating a structure that minimizes the bias or makes it completely transparent. I have attempted to do both in the following pages.

Finally, if polling is to be believed, most readers have already made up their minds. This book may well be an affront to your sensibilities and foregone conclusions. Yet if you are still with me this far, then I must trust to your own fairness as I play out the rest of the analysis.

With all of that in mind, the goal of this section is to provide a set of moral and ethical models to serve as an unbiased structure and to apply them in an open, transparent, fact-based manner that will allow you to do the same (or not) as you so desire. You will get my opinion and see how it is developed, but you don't have to accept it. You will be able to adjust how you weigh the facts and then reapply the model yourself. You will also have the power to apply a different model. The power to decide is yours

Let's start with a set of moral and ethical frameworks that can be used to complete a moral analysis of the practice of offshore outsourcing.

CHAPTER 21

Moral Frameworks

FINDING AN INITIAL SET of moral and ethical models that can be used for an analysis of outsourcing is straightforward even for a novice in the area of ethics and moral philosophy. The power of Google led me almost immediately to Santa Clara University's Markkula Center for Applied Ethics. Considering Santa Clara University is a Jesuit university in the heart of Silicon Valley and the Jesuits typically put a real emphasis on ethics and morality, this seemed a fitting place to start.

The Markkula Center's website[1] details a set of ethical models and a basic approach to identifying and reaching a decision on an ethical and moral dilemma.[2] I recommend you look at this material for yourself, but I'll briefly paraphrase a few illustrative steps in the process.

Recognize an Ethical Issue

To determine if you have an ethical or moral issue on your hands, start with some basic questions like:
- Is something wrong either personally or socially?
- Does the situation cause harm to people or communities?
- Does the issue go beyond legal or organizational concerns?
- Does it hurt people's dignity or hopes for a better life?[3]

In the case of outsourcing, the answers to the questions above clearly trend to the yes. Most people consider the practice wrong socially and individually. It can cause harm to people and communities, and the issue extends beyond purely legalistic or business concerns. People who lose their jobs can face a protracted struggle to make ends meet and recover, severely impacting their hopes for a financially stable life.

Another question ethical literature often poses is whether you feel comfortable discussing the issue in front of friends and family. Outsourcing is a highly emotional topic. The times I've mentioned it in front of people at a happy hour or a dinner party, the instantaneous negative reaction is apparent. As a result, I find I have a tendency to self-censor and to describe the work I do to strangers in more general terms—IT consulting—another indication of a moral issue.

Based on this brief diagnostic, outsourcing easily qualifies as a moral issue.

Get the Facts

The next step in the process is to get the facts. This is what the first half of this book has been about. In the debate today, many people are throwing out opinions without knowing the facts. Most of what passes for dialogue on the topic of outsourcing is purely emotive—opinions without any underlying analytical rigor or sincere effort to discern the truth. This book has attempted to fill that gap.

The process we have gone through in the first two parts has been to collect as many facts on both sides of the cost-benefit equation and to quantify their impact as impartially as possible. Such impacts represent the fallout of the outsourcing decision through a chain of events flowing directly and indirectly (or feeding back) through the economy, politics, and society.

Assessment

Assessment is where we get down to action. Here, we utilize various moral and ethical decision models to determine how they apply to the problem at hand.

The first step is to choose an ethical model. The options to choose from include:

Utilitarian Approach

In the Utilitarian model, an ethical decision is the one that will produce the greatest balance of benefits over harms, meaning more people benefit than get hurt. The challenge in this model is to include all the costs and benefits and to weight these in a way that is fair and impartial. The strength of this model is that it is relatively easy to use and has the potential to be less subjective than others.

Rights Approach

In the Rights approach, the ethical decision is the one that best respects the rights of all affected by a given decision or action. With this model, not everyone may get all they want, but the key question is whether everyone's rights and dignity are respected along the way and throughout the process. The key challenge with this model is that different parties to an action may have very different perceptions about what affronts their dignity and what constitutes their rights.

Fairness or Justice Approach

In the Fairness or Justice model, the goal is to assess whether a given decision or issue treats all stakeholders equally, or if unequally, that people are treated proportionately and fairly. This idea may be attractive for those who believe companies have a duty to meet the needs of all their stakeholders including employees, shareholders, and the larger community. Its weakness, however, is that there is no complete consensus in our society about what companies' responsibilities in this area are.

Common Good Approach

In the Common Good model, the goal is to determine if the issue or decision contributes most to the achievement of a quality common life together. In other words, which option would help all citizens participate more fully in the life we share as a family, community, and society? This model has similar issues to the Fairness and Justice model. These revolve around the question of how and where to draw the line when there are significant disagreements about what constitutes the common good and how best to achieve it. Liberals and conservatives often have diametrically opposing points of view on this topic, which means applying this model involves taking a side.

Virtue Approach

The Virtue model makes it personal. It puts the onus on the decision maker by asking the question of whether or not you would want to be the sort of person who acts this way. The value in this model is that decisions are personal, and they come down to real people. And some decisions involve life-and-death outcomes that should be well within the boundaries of morality for even the most ruthless CEO. But virtue is in the eye of the beholder and highly subjective in many cases.

Summary

Elements of each framework are applicable, yet each presents challenges. In a classic ethical decision process, you would assess the decision to be made using each of the models and then determine your course of action based on what they collectively tell you. However, in reviewing the models presented here for their applicability to the topic of outsourcing, Utilitarianism is perhaps the best fit, as it allows the most objective weighing of costs and benefits. It also fits into the goal of this book, which is to determine to what extent people have benefited or been harmed both at home and abroad as a result of outsourcing.

Simplicity is a virtue. A straightforward cost-benefit analysis allows more transparency and flexibility for readers to construct and deconstruct a point of view for themselves. If you can see how each cost or benefit is added up, then you are armed with the knowledge to analyze the math yourself. New data, new studies, and new headlines pop up daily, so the results can change with new information. Presenting the Utilitarian method as a framework allows readers to reapply the ethical analysis structure to reach new conclusions as the available information changes.

Utilitarianism, however, is not perfect or right in all cases. For instance, in the debate about the use of torture on suspected terrorists, utilitarianism may lead us astray. Harming—torturing—one or a few individuals to safeguard the welfare of many thousands or millions seems an attractive case from a utilitarian perspective. That does not mean it is the right thing to do.

While Utilitarianism is not right for all moral and ethical decisions, it does seem well suited for a discussion of costs and benefits as they relate to outsourcing, and it should help us determine if more people win than lose.

It's now time to apply the model.

CHAPTER 22

The Moral Case on Outsourcing

THE COSTS AND BENEFITS of outsourcing have been explored in the earlier parts and chapters of this book. Then we reviewed a set of moral and ethical frameworks for assessing an issue. Now we'll apply what we have found across the costs and benefits that have been discussed, starting with job loss.

Job Loss

Net job loss compares the cost of jobs lost from outsourcing against the benefits of jobs gained from outsourcing. The data is not complete, but the pattern seems clear. Job loss directly caused by outsourcing appears to be currently running in the range of 450,000 to 550,000 jobs each year across the services and manufacturing sectors combined.

I've tried to estimate on the high side throughout the analysis, but my personal experience may be of interest. In my career, I have had just one role in which I directly managed the transfer of jobs from the United States to India. It involved twenty IT jobs at a client in the San Francisco Bay area. I approached it with a great deal of angst. What I found, however, was that eighteen out of the twenty people who were losing their jobs were Indian nationals on H1B visas. Just two were American citizens. In effect, I took jobs away from Indian nationals working temporarily in the United States and transferred them to Indian nationals in India. To my knowledge, all these workers, including the two Americans, were able to find new jobs.

I offer this anecdote not to excuse or apologize for the jobs lost in the United States, but to explain my bias in this area. My personal experience leads me to suspect that the true impact of job loss in the

United States may be smaller than even my own estimate above, which is intentionally conservative—biased to the high side—for the purposes of fairly evaluating the data.

No matter what the number, job loss from outsourcing is not small in absolute terms. There is always a cost. Real people get hurt when they lose their jobs, and not everyone is able to bounce back easily and find new employment. However, layoffs as a result of outsourcing are small in relation to total layoffs each year across the US economy. To put it in context, it appears to represent just 2 to 2.5 percent of total job loss from all layoffs for all reasons. The other 98 percent of involuntary layoffs and job separations each year across the US economy are not caused by outsourcing, but by something else (an issue we will come back to in the final section).

Some job losses from outsourcing are offset by jobs gained directly or indirectly from trade related to outsourcing. The Business Roundtable analysis of Trade and American Jobs, using China trade as a proxy for outsourcing, provides a rough estimate for this factor. The numbers suggest that the United States gained 300,000 jobs each year between 2004 and 2008 from outsourcing-related imports and exports. This number may be conservative. The same study found total jobs gained from overall trade-related activity averaged 1.8 million jobs per year from 2004-2008. The total related to outsourcing may be much higher than my use of China as a proxy.

In addition, the United States benefits from foreign companies investing in the United States and insourcing jobs when they open offices and build factories instead of exporting from their home economies. This adds around 100,000 new jobs per year. To avoid double counting with the Business Roundtable's overall trade numbers (e.g., to factor out import and export trade-related jobs), I've discounted that number by 50 percent to 50,000 net jobs added per year.

Combining the estimated 450,000 to 550,000 jobs lost from outsourcing per year with the estimate of 350,000 jobs gained per year yields a net job loss from outsourcing in America today of somewhere in the range of 100,000 to 200,000 jobs lost per year.

Middle-Class Anxiety: Wages & Costs

Wage stagnation is often linked in the popular press to trade, globalization, and outsourcing. However, the data reviewed earlier suggests that offshore outsourcing appears to play a small role in the dilemma of stagnating wages faced by American workers over the last decade. Most studies suggest that it is not the largest influence on lowering wages for American workers, even from left-leaning think tanks. One book, *Blue-Collar Blues*, finds that the impact was heaviest prior to 2000 and was minimal even then.

There are other reasons for wage stagnation. A McKinsey Global Institute analysis found that the biggest issue is an overabundance of low-skill Americans competing for low-wage, low-skill jobs, thereby pushing down wages for everyone in this part of the economy. The 30 percent of people with higher skills are getting a wage premium precisely because these higher skills are in relative short supply.

There is also anecdotal evidence to suggest that non-wage compensation in the form of higher health care costs paid by employers has displaced some of what could have been wage increases for workers across all skill categories.

On the positive side, however, outsourcing has played a small role in increasing incomes for people in some industries such as agriculture and mining and technology firms, including innovation jobs at companies that specialize in product design, development, and marketing. However, there is little data to quantify this positive effect, and it appears to impact a relatively smaller portion of workers overall.

Conventional wisdom suggests that wages have stagnated because of greater globalization and outsourcing. However, analytical proof to support the suggestion that outsourcing is the primary or even a major cause of US wage stagnation is lacking. And there is a long list of other suspects, ranging from poor skill levels to high health care costs.

Overall, my bias remains to weight the net impact on wages due to outsourcing as slightly negative, albeit not one that we are able to quantify.

Bad Products vs. Consumer Savings

Over the last few years, Americans have seen a slew of recalls and warnings regarding products that are dangerous to consumers. Many companies have outsourced production without adequately testing the quality of what their suppliers ship them, or they are complicit in turning a blind eye. Companies put relentless pressure on their suppliers to cut costs. The combination of pressure on costs without testing for quality leads—unsurprisingly—to corners getting cut, sometimes with harmful or fatal results.

Despite all the issues with lower-quality goods, it is hard to objectively quantify the overall impact of this problem or to know its true extent. We would need to know the actual risks and to differentiate between cheaper goods—ones that consumers choose to purchase knowing they are not the same quality as premium-priced products—versus dangerous products, such as toys tainted with lead that can cause actual injury. I know no source of data that has done this and so leave the cost side of this equation as unquantified for now.

The benefit side, however, is easier to quantify. We saw earlier that there is a range of savings to consumers from outsourcing to low-cost providers in other countries. For trade overall, the savings are in the range of $3,000 to $5,000 per individual and $7,000 to $12,000 per household. Outsourcing is a component of trade and so contributes to these numbers. Walmart by itself has been estimated to generate annual savings to consumers of $1,000 per individual and $2,500 per household.

Using the Walmart numbers as a proxy for outsourcing's impact (noting that Walmart is just one of many big-box retailers that presumably affect the economy in similar ways), the net impact is consumer savings of $1,000 per individual and $2,500 per household, partially offset in an unquantified amount by the risks posed by lower-quality, dangerous products.

Labor Exploitation vs. Migrant Opportunity

Most people cry foul when they see or read about working conditions in Chinese factories—the long hours, the crowded factory dorms, the dangerous working conditions that can result in injury or worse. The evidence I have seen overwhelmingly points to the fact that labor exploitation and abuses are rampant throughout the manufacturing side of the industry. China looms large in this picture given the vast size of its export sector, which is almost entirely built on outsourcing. However, similar conditions are found in any developing country—as well as in a few developed ones.

Recent scandals have dominated press coverage. An example is the worker suicides at Foxconn's massive factories in China in the early summer of 2010 mentioned earlier. (The result was a doubling of wages by the company while under intense media scrutiny.)

The overall picture of worker exploitation appears to be changing with revised labor laws introduced in 2008, increasing awareness of workers' rights, a restive workforce willing to strike (and litigate), and demographic changes that are slowly, ever so slowly, changing the balance of power between companies and employees. But there have been, and remain, abuses and bad working conditions, and these are endemic, resulting from the way outsourcing as an industry operates.

There is, however, the counter perspective of the opportunities that are created for rural migrants who aspire to a better life and a pathway out of rural poverty. Migrants seek jobs in the big city and the assembly line is the first step in a career ladder—a step up from low-paying farmwork. Many never get beyond that first rung, but some do. Life in a factory is not fun. There is a terrible price to pay on many dimensions, including the impact on families that are split up and children left behind. But it is a huge mistake to think these are not desirable jobs for millions of people whose alternative is rural village life.

This is not to excuse the poor and dangerous working conditions that are found at most factories. Or the low wages, the lack of bathroom breaks, or the lack of employment contracts. It does not excuse the factory boss for wringing everything he can out of his or her workers against the letter or spirit of local laws. It certainly does not excuse the American importer who shrugs off the poor working conditions because it is inconvenient to notice and would cut into profit margins to do something about it.

The industry is responsible for the working conditions it imposes and perpetuates. For that reason, I believe the overall impact of labor exploitation in the context of outsourcing is negative. But my bias is not to forget that millions of people living in rural villages are eager for the chance to migrate to the city to work in factories and have effectively voted with their feet. Activists should keep working to make this experience safe and fair for them.

Environment

China's export sector is—as we have seen—massive. It is largely driven by outsourcing. Chinese officials, themselves, have suggested that 15 to 25 percent of their country's total pollution is caused by the outsourcing of Western production to China. This amounts to between 1 and 2 billion tons of carbon dioxide emitted each year, specifically tied to outsourcing, contributing a tangible volume to the problem of global warming.

What is also true, however, is that this production would have used energy and produced greenhouse gases if it were carried out at home. However, it might have used more efficient and less polluting sources of energy, so I have estimated the net contribution of outsourcing production to China as ranging from 25 to 50 percent of the total, or 500 million to 1 billion tons of greenhouse gases each year. I'll use this figure as the proxy for the environmental damage caused by outsourcing as an industry.

Unfair Competition

There is an ongoing debate about whether countries, primarily China, are competing unfairly with an undervalued exchange rate, pervasive government subsidies and support, and lax regulatory enforcement that, combined, result in exports that steal markets and jobs from more advanced countries.

The answer seems obvious: China is neo-mercantilist and a currency manipulator. As of the spring of 2011, some estimates placed the fair value of the Chinese currency 24 percent higher than its rate at that time. China is likely to devalue its currency only gradually, and so the exchange rate will continue to drive tensions in the US–China relationship. China also has a pervasive web of state subsidies and support for exporters, which are clearly unfair by the letter and spirit of the country's WTO agreement.

But China also follows smart policies and aggressively makes the infrastructure and educational investments that are helping it to increase economic growth. Nor are Chinese suppliers and entrepreneurs standing still. They are willing to go to great lengths to gain business, cutting deals at very low margins, working hard to improve productivity, and quickly innovating across the board. This type of competition is entirely fair and does not get enough attention, although it has negative implications for Western companies that are not as dynamic or aggressive in their willingness to compete and grow.

How, then, do all these factors sum up in the moral case on outsourcing? Job loss and labor exploitation are already accounted for in our framework, and it would be unfair to double count these. For now, there is no readily apparent way to quantify an incremental impact from unfair competition. Therefore, I will retain a negative bias for this section, meaning I readily acknowledge that there is some negative impact from unfair competition. Outsourcing as an industry has some level of responsibility for this negative impact, and that is above and beyond factors such as job loss and labor exploitation that have already been considered.

Buying America

Inward foreign direct investment creates both jobs and fears in America. There are some buyers we fear, namely those from China and the Middle East. These are the groups that are accumulating vast hoards of dollars and need to invest that money somewhere. Yet we have little trust about their intentions and whether they would exercise commercial interests or political influence over what they buy.

Broadly speaking, however, foreign investment in the United States creates and sustains jobs here. Today, more than 5 million jobs are supported by foreign companies that have invested in America. More is set to come.

Here again, China is a good proxy for the impact related to outsourcing. John Watkins of the American Chamber of Commerce in China has spoken of the potential for Chinese foreign direct investments to reach $1 trillion in the United States by 2030. This would almost certainly result in the creation of millions of American jobs, a process just beginning. Watkins isn't alone. The Asia Society has also suggested that Chinese companies will invest more than $1 trillion overseas by 2020, much of which could be in the United States.

To date, China is believed to invest as much as 60 to 70 percent of its accumulated foreign exchange reserves via purchases of US Treasury Bills. This has served to keep Americans' borrowing costs low on everything from mortgage debt to consumer loans. This is saving US citizens, both as consumers and taxpayers, hundreds or even thousands of dollars per person per year in lower interest rates on everything from personal loans to government interest expenses now and in the future. China loses money on this deal every time it has to appreciate the yuan. Over time, the country may lose hundreds of billions of dollars on what it has invested.

Outsourcing has been the primary mechanism for China's accumulation of reserves and for the success of its companies, which are now poised to invest in the United States to be closer to their customers. The political fears regarding China's foreign direct investments in America, while easy to fan, are unsubstantiated. The benefits of investment in the United States, either financially or through foreign direct investment, are overwhelmingly positive for American consumers and taxpayers.

Poverty

Poverty is the trump card in my personal moral analysis. For me, poverty is the sound of wailing in the night. Living in a small village in Africa as a Peace Corps volunteer, it was a sound I heard all too often.

It starts as single mournful wail of anguish, a lone voice crying out loss and pain. A child has died—or a brother, a parent, perhaps a sister. In a village, the anguish quickly spreads and finds an echoing response. And then another and another. Soon wailing carries from all directions as the village women converge—no matter the hour—to share in the grief and to provide comfort.

There is nothing romantic about poverty, especially its rural variant. It is measured in shorter lives, wasted potential, and a stifling lack of opportunity. This is where outsourcing comes in. By all measures, outsourcing has had an extraordinary impact on reducing extreme poverty in East Asia, primarily in China. Nearly 500 million Chinese have been lifted out of extreme poverty in less than a generation. This is surely one of the most underreported, historic events in human history, and it has barely registered on the Western conscience. Nevertheless, it is true.

What has driven this huge, historic drop in poverty rates? Because exports are dominated by outsourcing, as we have seen, and exports account for nearly 40 percent of Chinese GDP, then the direct impact of outsourcing has been to employ more than 100 million Chinese workers, lifting many of these people out of extreme poverty. It is also the foundation of an indirect multiplier effect that is driving the massive construction and infrastructure boom, thus creating another large portion of Chinese GDP and employing hundreds of millions more people. These massive economic forces are not only lifting people out of poverty in China, but all around the world. India has also seen 2 million jobs created in its services outsourcing industry with four times that supported indirectly.

The decision to outsource is based on a business case that is driven by a company's self-interest and profit margins. These decisions have nothing to do with altruistic goals, yet they are driving a massive reduction in poverty. Love it or hate it, outsourcing appears to have contributed more to China's shift away from poverty in a shorter time than any Western development effort has during the last fifty years anywhere in the world. It has directly and indirectly benefited approximately 500 million people.

Chapter 23

Summary: The Utilitarian Case

THERE IS ROOM for disagreement. My biases are on display in how I have weighted the various dimensions of cost and benefit from jobs to poverty reduction, environmental pollution to labor exploitation. You can disagree or rearrange the pieces we have discussed, but here is my personal summary of the issues and their net negative or positive impact:

Job loss and wage stagnation are the biggest fears that most Americans share about outsourcing, yet the evidence suggests a very small impact in net terms. This is true both in absolute numbers as well as relative to the size of our economy and the other forces at work. Job loss may even be in positive territory depending on how inclusive we are about trade-related jobs (running at roughly +1.8 million per year from 2004 to 2008). Overall, these costs appear to be minimal across the US economy (although not at the individual level to people who have lost a job or communities that have been decimated by a plant closure).

The annual savings we as consumers accumulate from outsourcing are estimated at $2,500 per household. This is tangible savings, and the real number could be even more. We enjoy additional benefits from the financial flows that hold down the interest rates on our mortgages, credit cards, and other debts (it also gives us the often-abused chance to increase personal debt) even as we worry about foreign governments buying America.

The case for unfair competition is valid. From exchange rates to subsidies, China is aggressively building markets and promoting exports. Not all of this has to do with outsourcing, however, and it is unclear if any additional impact on jobs can be quantified.

Labor exploitation is an endemic problem, and the industry, both on the supplier and buyer sides, is clearly complicit in the problem. Yet exploitation must be juxtaposed with the opportunity it has given to rural migrants to move to the city and earn a higher income. This benefit is real, and outsourcing has been the mechanism for creating this opportunity.

Outsourcing is also at the heart of the biggest human transformation in history, the lifting of 500 million people out of poverty in East Asia, predominantly China.

The bottom line for me comes down to this: There are large benefits to Americans as a result of outsourcing. The costs are relatively small, manageable, and largely offset by the gains. Overseas, the benefits appear to heavily outweigh the costs despite some of the serious issues that need to be resolved, from environmental pollution to labor exploitation.

Future benefits are hard to quantify. If China is able to shift from an export-centric economy to a consumption-oriented one, a move potentially necessitated by international pressure and China's own internal desire to continue growing, then the future benefits may well be even greater.

All of this flies in the face of conventional wisdom, and you don't have to take what I have laid out here as the final, conclusive result. You should think it through for yourself. I reevaluate the framework every time I read the headlines. I find myself sifting and considering new facts all the time. I go back and forth about China and whether or not we will be able to compete. I worry about the structure of job loss and whether or not the relatively small percentage caused by outsourcing overall actually impacts more or less in smaller slices of the economy. I hunt for new insights—negative or positive—that will impact the big picture.

Despite these nagging worries, this is where I stand now, based on where the facts seem to fall and what I have learned to date. It is an imperfect conclusion, but it seems the fairest one to make given the facts as I know them. The utilitarian model would say a decision is moral if there are more benefits for more people than there are harms and people harmed. In this case, outsourcing—despite its issues—appears to be in positive territory for both Americans and the rest of the world.

Regardless of what appears to be a generally positive net picture both at home and abroad, I am not assuming most readers will accept this argument or change their opinion, even if they actually were to agree on all the individual facts and how I have assessed them. That is why I wanted to put my conclusions to the test. I had a plan for doing so: the Campfire Test.

CHAPTER 24

The Campfire Test

FROM A UTILITARIAN perspective, it would appear that the costs weighed against the benefits of outsourcing lean toward the positive. If this is true, is shifting conventional wisdom simply a matter of showing people the pros and cons and how they stack up? I had doubts. I decided to give my thesis a sanity check, which I called the Campfire Test.

Here is how it works: Set up a weekend camping trip with some of your best buddies. Make sure you do at least one rigorous full-day hike, preferably up a mountain and back. After the hike, grill up steaks and roast potatoes over a campfire. Wash it down with plenty of beer. Later, sit around a campfire jawboning with scotch and cigars. Take that moment to pitch your book. Walk through the costs and the benefits. Make a clear, rational argument that outsourcing is likely to be positive. One might expect smart, rational people—or at least your best friends—to humor you and accept a well-reasoned and brilliantly pitched case.

But alas, this is not what happened. My points were soundly rejected. My friends simply could not believe that the positive dimensions were true. Or at least that is how I recall it.

What surprised me at the time was that facts didn't matter to my friends—friends, for the record, who are fairly smart, well-grounded people. There are times when I hold my own in a debate, and in such cases the ability to marshall facts confers a big advantage. This time was different. The facts that I presented went against the grain of all that my friends believed to be true.

Now, to be fair to my friends, I was almost certainly not as eloquent or reasonable after a big hike and an evening of steaks, beer, and scotch as I like to remember and portray. It's possible my recollection is not entirely to be trusted. But the experience (and memory) are accurate enough to offer some potential insights. And these are worrisome. The reality is that facts are not persuasive, and this is an important clue to the underlying dynamics that make this issue so deeply volatile and emotional.

Something more elemental and instinctive is at play. And it has a lot to do with morality. Emotion and instinct frequently defy logic when it comes to something as bedrock as morality—and its application to the moral case on outsourcing. And that leads us to the Trolley Car Problem to explain what is going on.

Chapter 25

The Trolley Car Problem

THE TROLLEY CAR problem comes up in almost any book, essay, or article involving current research on moral philosophy. It is one of the tools used by researchers to gain insights and evidence on how we process moral decisions.

The Trolley Car scenario goes like this: One day while walking over a bridge, you see a trolley car racing out of control down the track and the driver slumped over the controls or, in some versions, missing entirely. Farther down the tracks, five workers are doing maintenance on the tracks with their backs turned, unaware of the approaching danger. You are standing at a juncture in the tracks. If you pull a lever, it will divert the trolley car down a separate track. You will save the lives of five men. But there is one man working on the other line who will be killed. Is it okay to pull the switch to save five, knowing your action will kill one?

Most people presented with this dilemma answer yes, that it is okay to pull the switch and save five lives. This is fairly straightforward. Switch pulling is morally acceptable.

However, consider another version of this scenario. Once again you see a trolley car running out of control, and if it isn't stopped or diverted, five men will die. But this time you are standing next to a fat man on a bridge. The only way to stop the trolley car is to push the man off the bridge in front of the car. His body on the tracks will stop the car, but he will be killed. Is it okay to push the man off the bridge to save the five?

Most people answer no to this second scenario. And this is where it gets interesting.

Technically speaking, the utilitarian calculation is exactly the same. One person dies, five are saved. From a purely utilitarian perspective, the outcomes are the same, so the answer should be as well. But it isn't.

People view the choices differently. The switch pull is impersonal and moral, but man-handling someone and causing direct harm is not.

Why the disconnect? A new branch of moral philosophy called Moral Foundations Theory offers a potential explanation for what's going on.

Chapter 26

Moral Foundations Theory

A GROWING SCHOOL of thought attempts to integrate recent findings across such seemingly diverse fields as evolutionary psychology, neuroscience, and moral philosophy. The unifying idea is that humans reach moral judgments not through an objective analysis of facts but instinctively based on a common set of moral principles, or building blocks, that have essentially been hardwired into the human brain through evolution from the very early days of the human race. The theory that has evolved around this concept is called Moral Foundations Theory, and its pioneers are Jonathan Haidt, Jesse Graham, and their colleagues.[4]

The underlying idea behind Moral Foundations Theory involves intuitions and how judgments and ideas pop into our head in reaction to almost any situation. Moral intuitions are those instincts that specifically focus on feelings related to approval or disapproval about the situations we see. Haidt and colleagues focused on scenarios that created strong feelings of disapproval—to the point of disgust—ranging from incestuous relations to eating the pet dog. The scenarios are all essentially more provocative versions of the Trolley Car Problem. The sum of all this research is that people generate near instantaneous intuitive reactions to moral and ethical problems.

Until recently, moral reasoning was generally seen as a deliberative process by which people analyzed moral and ethical dilemmas and then reasoned their way to moral judgments. Intuitions were seen in a supporting or peripheral role. There was just one problem: research was showing that people facing a dilemma made quick gut reactions, deciding their opinion within a second or two. Then, when forced to explain how they reached their decision, these same people in effect searched for evidence that supported the point of view they had already reached.

Instead of acting like wise judges deliberately weighing the pros and cons of a dilemma, people were actually acting the part of lawyers, working to marshal facts to support their case and discarding those facts that did not fit. This was a process of rationalizing a moral judgment already made, not a deliberate reasoning process to arrive at a moral judgment.

In his book *Human*, Michael Gozzaniga describes the evolutionary adaptations that might have led to such moral intuitions. They might have derived from the early days of the human race when the primary social units were small hunter-gatherer groups. Humans had to learn how to trust each other, how to rear children, how to cooperate. This probably took untold thousands of years of trial and error in which evolution rewarded those who were good at socializing and working together to survive and slowly weeded out those who were not. At the individual level, what resulted were gut instincts about how to behave and how to judge whether someone else was behaving appropriately at a time when language was rudimentary at best.[5]

We carry those genes with us today, hardwired into the fiber of our being. Like it or not, we are still the product of those early human creatures struggling to survive in small groups against terrifying odds. The sophisticated breadth of language, civilization, and advanced knowledge characteristic of the human species today are all relatively recent phenomena, barely processed as yet by the powerful forces of evolutionary selection and the aeons of time.

That brings us back to Moral Foundations Theory. The theory proposed by Haidt and Graham is that moral intuitions are processed based on five foundational building blocks. These are described on the *www.moralfoundations.org* website. (You can also contribute to scientific research by taking your own online tests on morality, ethics, and values at *www.yourmorals.org* and find out, among other things, if you are as liberal or conservative as you think.)

The five moral foundations are:

- *Harm/Care:* A dislike for seeing others in pain. This foundation is the basis for kindness, gentleness, etc.
- *Fairness/Reciprocity:* An approval of people who reciprocate favors and a disapproval of cheaters. This is the foundation strongly linked

to concepts of justice, rights, etc.

- *Ingroup/Loyalty*: A foundation that provides strong identity and loyalty to a group and leads to feelings of patriotism and self-sacrifice.
- *Authority/Respect*: An approval of respect for authority, traditions, and deferring to those in charge and a disapproval of followers who violate or dismiss authority as well as leaders who misuse their role. This foundation is derived from the hierarchical structure of the small, early hunter-gatherer groups.
- *Purity/Sanctity*: An approval of purity and cleanliness built around concepts of disgust and contamination. This foundational value undergirds religious beliefs.

The Moral Foundations Theory proposes that these basic building blocks within our brains are the automatic processors, the metaphoric internal chips, with which we reach gut-based, moral intuitions that instantly take shape as moral judgments.

Not only do we reach intuitions first and then rationalize them second, it is apparently very hard to override moral intuitions once made. In some cases, social interaction and group conformity may help influence our beliefs, albeit in a surprisingly small way. In other cases, where a person has exceptional powers of logic and the moral intuition is not overly strong, a person may override intuition to reach a new moral judgment. Again, it is rare.

An interesting offshoot of Haidt's research is that there are differences between liberals and conservatives in how they reach moral judgments. Liberals tend to react most strongly around the moral foundations of Harm/Care and Fairness/Reciprocity. Conservatives tend to weight all five of the moral foundations more equally. This plays out in the positions we take on politically divisive issues. There is a moral structure to most issues, and recent research postulates that Moral Foundations Theory may help explain some of the differences in how conservative and liberals react to such issues.

An example is illegal immigration. Opposition to illegal immigration appears related to a higher emphasis on the Authority/Respect and Purity/Sanctity modules. This seems to suggest that the socially conservative position is concerned that immigrants will subvert American traditions (authority) and bring in polluting foreign elements (purity). By contrast, supporters of immigration are more focused on Harm/Care, implying that supporters are basing their position on compassion for the poor.[6] The example of illegal immigration is just one politically sensitive issue that shows how people react differently based on moral foundations.

But the implications are significant. People approach a political discussion instinctively looking for facts to support their point of view rather than objectively considering all facts. This makes the opportunity to change people's opinions quite narrow.

What, then, does Moral Foundations Theory suggest about how people feel about outsourcing? Hint: it's not good news for the industry.

CHAPTER 27

Moral Foundations and Outsourcing

ALTHOUGH THIS introduction to Moral Foundations Theory is basic (on par with my own understanding), it does suggest solid reasons why outsourcing and the offshoring of American jobs have little hope of gaining support from Americans. Ever. Simply put, it violates too many of the basic moral foundations to have a chance. This is bad news for businesspeople and an easy target for politicians to attack.

It seems clear that the outsourcing of jobs creates a strong sense of disapproval based on at least three of the moral foundations.

Harm/Care

The offshoring of jobs almost certainly resonates with people as a violation of the Harm/Care principle. It hurts people and communities. We know this from the stories we see in the press. Whether it's a plant closure or a round of corporate layoffs, what the media reports and what is reinforced by what we see and experience is the impact to workers who have lost their jobs. This is the human dimension, and it is an overwhelmingly powerful part of the story.

The pain and human suffering associated with job loss inspires an instinctive and spontaneous feeling of empathy for the victims (immediate, tangible) and disapproval toward those that have caused it (remote, faceless). The moral foundation of Harm/Care is one of the most powerful underlying building blocks upon which moral intuitions are made. It would clearly elicit a viscerally negative reaction to the idea of outsourcing.

In fact, the idea that many if not most job losses or plant closures have something to do with jobs going offshore has become deeply ingrained in the public psyche, even though it actually represents just 2 percent of total jobs lost each year. The idea of offshore outsourcing has been deeply acculturated as something that causes harm to people, workers, and communities on a broad scale.

Fairness/Reciprocity

Offshoring also touches on the moral foundation of Fairness/Reciprocity in several ways. For a generation, we have seen a growing split between the corporate elites who are commanding ever-higher salaries and the workers that are facing the brunt of wage stagnation and job loss. When a factory closes, it seems grossly unfair that CEOs and shareholders profit as employees are cast aside like discarded refuse. The storyline that there is a causal and unfair relationship between factory closures and rising CEO pay and stock prices is also one that has become deeply ingrained in the American psyche.

There is another dimension to the Fairness/Reciprocity foundation. That is the fundamental belief that when multinational corporations move jobs offshore, they are doing so to exploit labor overseas and to destroy the environment. These issues come up again and again in the context of trade treaties. Opponents lean heavily on the idea that countries overseas do not have fair labor laws or practices, environmental safeguards, or safety standards. The multinationals that take jobs to these countries are exploiting the lack of such standards. Countries that do not have these measures in place are either being taken advantage of or are competing unfairly.

For these reasons, offshoring jobs is almost certain to inspire an instinctive gut reaction as grossly unfair.

Ingroup/Loyalty

The third moral foundation that comes strongly into play around the concept of outsourcing is Ingroup/Loyalty. If the theory is right, we are hardwired from early in our evolution to be loyal to our immediate tribe and to rely on a small group of people within our immediate vicinity for survival. It is hard for Americans (or anyone else in the same situation, for that matter) to accept jobs going overseas to people who are not of the same tribe—in this case, Americans. It's a fundamental violation of the basic premise of Ingroup/Loyalty.

We instinctively identify with people closer to home. We are members of a family unit, a community, a tribe, a nation. Much farther down the list come human beings in another country far removed from our own, especially if they have different accents, features, and mannerisms.

In a shallow way, this appears to be prejudice against accents, ethnicities, and different cultures. Yet, in the example of a conversation with a call center representative with a foreign accent, a negative reaction may simply involve an elemental gut reaction as people intuitively sense a violation of Ingroup/Loyalty. A job lost here is one taken from our group. Offshoring, therefore, is a betrayal of Ingroup/Loyalty, and when it occurs, it will invariably spark gut-level disapproval.

Summary

At a minimum, the three moral foundations of Harm/Car, Fairness/ Reciprocity, and Ingroup/Loyalty come into play on the topic of the outsourcing and whether it is morally acceptable or not. All three foundations most likely underlie strong disapproval. It is no wonder that our moral instincts can and are strongly aroused by the very idea of outsourcing jobs to other countries.

The involvement of three moral foundations also suggests that both liberals and conservatives should have nearly identical reactions against offshoring. And that seems to hold up in the numbers we noted earlier, which show an overwhelming consensus within the public that outsourcing is a bad thing that hurts Americans.

Even though a case exists that the benefits of outsourcing outweigh the costs in a strictly utilitarian analysis, most people feel an intuitive connection to people like ourselves who are being harmed whereas those who benefit appear to be very different from us—a small group of corporate executives in this country or a large group of people in other countries who are not a recognizable part of our own community.

So where does that leave us?

The conclusions are sobering. They suggest that improving the image of outsourcing will never be just an exercise in public education. In fact, it may never really be possible. Moral intuitions are arrayed against this issue, and moral intuitions are very, very hard to override, no matter how well-educated people are.

That said, there are some elements of the theory and its application to outsourcing that I struggle with. The data seems to suggest that outsourcing directly affects a relatively minor part of the American workforce and that it has touched far fewer people than is anecdotally believed. Yet most people have an overwhelming feeling that outsourcing is having a disproportionate or even overwhelming impact on American jobs. How did Americans become so deeply worried about outsourcing? Why aren't we more worried about technology-driven productivity changes? What explains the depth of intensity and the breadth of awareness?

Moral intuitions may explain the gut instinct, the negative reaction, but they do not explain this underlying level of intensity or awareness. How did we suddenly decide foreigners were to blame for every lost job? The intensity of the reaction seems out of context. And it is to context that I turn next.

CHAPTER 28

Narrative Bias

CONTEXT MATTERS.

I think of it as playing out in the form of a narrative bias that acts as an amplifier or dampener on our moral instincts, serving to either dial up or down the intensity of the reactions that people feel, at least in the case of politically divisive issues. A narrative bias, in effect, may act as a form of middle layer that helps interpret the signals that people are processing.

For example, in the early human hunter-gatherer groups, a small act of selfishness might have had very different repercussions depending on the context in which it occurred. Consider if a man was noticed taking an extra piece of meat for himself at the expense of someone else when a new kill was being divided up. He might well have suffered a severe penalty like ostracism in one context or merely been given a disapproving look and a shrug in another. The context and result would have depended on whether food was in short supply and group members were on the edge of starvation, or everyone was well-fed and the group was sitting on a big stock of meat. Petty selfishness is worthy of a passing glance of contempt. Stealing scarce resources that might endanger another's survival is something far more serious.

In the modern sense, an equivalent narrative bias might be an accumulated set of anecdotes that describes—or explains—the context of our times. This would be represented by the stock of media and political imagery, of mentally recorded sound bites and stories that highlight issues and reinforce a general perception of where we stand as a nation (or Ingroup) at a point in time. In America today, the narrative bias might be something akin to a once well-fed tribe now hungry and foraging for increasingly scarce game with a drought on the horizon and an impending sense of doom.

Put another way, the loss of a job matters little when the personal and economic harm is small and it is easy to jump to the next opportunity (akin to the tribe being well-fed and food stored up). It is a different matter when losing a job is catastrophic and imperils ones health care, house, family unity, and sense of self-worth, especially when new jobs are either hard to find or present a big drop in wages and benefits.

Consider also that on the national level we have had two decades of middle-class anxiety. We have seen a generation of wage stagnation, a series of jobless recoveries, relentless and expanding foreign competition, a dramatic decline in union membership (thought to have been the bedrock of middle-class stability), a corresponding decline in manufacturing (itself a perceived icon of national strength), competing nations that are acting unfairly within the global system of free trade at our expense, declining economic power against a backdrop of short- and long-term fiscal crises, and an economic and political model that inspires doubt when compared to rising powers like China, India, and others. The list goes on and on. The severity of the Great Recession and the rapid leap in unemployment simply caps a longer list of ills that have been stored up and filling in the narrative. The anecdotal imagery of job loss, hardship, and competitive onslaught has become deeply acculturated in America today.

In contrast, what we see overseas in emerging countries like China is an increasingly optimistic population that has witnessed rapid growth and increasing prosperity in a generation. The skyline changes by the day. Change is tangible. China seems to be standing proud on the world stage. There is a Chinese Dream, and it is embodied in confidence about the country's future. They are building and doing big things. It is not perfect. There are issues. But progress is visible. It is not just talk.

This is the context within which our moral instincts are aroused and, I believe, amplified when it comes to job loss from outsourcing. This makes supporters of outsourcing easy prey for politicians willing to play to extremes on either side of the political divide. More banally, this is an easy storyline for the media to place their stories within, regardless of its accuracy.

The level of intensity of our moral intuitions and judgments matters. Narrative context can amplify or dampen them. Outsourcing, unfortunately for the industry, fits into the larger political, social, and economic narrative of our times. It has become a metaphor for our fears and a scapegoat for our failures.

CONCLUSION

IT IS EMOTIONAL. It is instinctive. It is messy. The word *outsourcing* conjures up all sorts of instant reactions. Americans are worried about it. Most people believe that outsourcing is a bad thing and that it is hurting our economy.

There is truth to all of this. Outsourcing does take jobs away from some communities. Real people and real communities lose. People get hurt. Outsourcing may not be to blame for the vast majority of jobs lost in the American economy every year, but it contributes its share.

But is it switch pulling or manhandling? Losing jobs disrupts people's lives and interrupts their careers, and this is harmful, but how does it compare with other moral and ethical business dilemmas that have been witnessed in recent years? Lots of business activities involve moral quandaries. Consider a few recent examples:

- A drug company withholds data about the side effects of a blockbuster drug, resulting in the potential death of dozens of patients.
- Mortgage companies lure people into home loans they can't afford; banks evict people without properly checking their facts.
- Government contractors supply trailers with formaldehyde permeating the walls to people displaced by Hurricane Katrina, despite the health risks and illegality.
- Health insurance companies run programs to deny claims and coverage when people get sick. It saves money, but it kills people. (This practice supposedly ended with 2010 health care legislation.)
- Food companies target children with marketing campaigns to buy sugary foods at a time when the nation is in the midst of an epidemic of childhood obesity and diabetes, diseases that reduce life spans by years.

- Yet another drug company chooses to withhold information about contamination in children's medication and delay a recall, despite the potential danger to children's health and lives.

On the scale of moral and ethical problems, outsourcing does not seem to compare. The costs are well-known. They include job loss, wage stagnation, labor exploitation, environmental damage, and bad, dangerous products to name just a few.

But outsourcing also has large benefits. It's an important mechanism for increasing service, cutting costs, and making businesses stronger. It helps companies prosper and thereby creates jobs. It allows executive teams—already stretched by a complex series of challenges—to focus on what is most important in their business—their core competencies. It allows them to build capabilities overseas in new markets that hold the key to future growth. It does not put lives at risk.

Social benefits range from consumer savings to better, more available services. We get jobs from insourcing and from trade (both from exports and imports). Companies that do well help deliver profits to shareholders' retirement accounts. In aggregate the industry has been one of the biggest drivers of one of the largest human changes in history, the vast reduction in extreme poverty of half a billion human beings in East Asia.

If we address the offshoring aspect of this debate exclusively in utilitarian terms, a simple cost-benefit analysis seems to suggest the benefits side wins. Of course, the reader could weigh the costs and benefits differently or new information could become available that swings the argument either way.

But this analysis may be largely immaterial.

People respond to issues based on fundamental moral instincts. These instincts suggest that outsourcing violates the moral foundations of Fairness/Reciprocity (CEOs benefit, workers get tossed aside), Harm/Care (workers and communities are hurt), and Ingroup/Loyalty (jobs go to other people, not our tribe).

Moral instincts are powerful. They are also fundamentally rooted to culture and context. Today's context is an acculturated sense of increasing vulnerability to job loss and the potential to fall out of the middle class entirely. It is my opinion that context does not change the instant moral reaction or tip the balance between how manhandling and switch pulling are perceived, but it does amplify the intensity that we feel about a given issue.

Thus here is the unsatisfying conclusion: outsourcing delivers significant benefits, but these cannot be accepted while the broader context is perceived to be so negative. For something like outsourcing to be tolerable, there needs to be a counter-narrative of anecdotal imagery and experience to suggest that the harm is limited, that fairness and reciprocity are involved, and that American communities and the nation as a whole can benefit and prosper. Changing the context requires nothing less than a program—a set of tangible policies and recommendations—that can be implemented and visibly demonstrate that America and Americans can prosper in an age of globalization, outsourcing, and rapid technology change. Remedying the current context is the focus of the final part of this book.

PART 4

REMEDIES

OVERVIEW

"MY KIDS ARE SCREWED."

I've been noticing this phrase a lot lately. It's often accompanied by a tone of resignation and a shake of the head. Sometimes it's preceded with the qualifier, "I'll be okay, but…" Sometimes it is not. The level of pessimism about the future is strikingly at odds with traditional American optimism. Something is seriously wrong, and it didn't just start with the Great Recession.

As if to capture the zeitgeist, the *Financial Times* ran a catchy story in 2010 titled, "Goodbye, American Dream." In it, the author profiles two American families struggling to make ends meet, and he puts these struggles in the context of a triple whammy hitting the great American middle class. The forces at work are declining median wages (people are earning less over time), declining social mobility (the chance to rise from poor to rich, the classic American Dream, is decreasing), and increasing inequality (the rich are getting a bigger share of national income).[1]

Any one of these trends alone would be grounds for concern. All are occurring simultaneously—and have been for a generation.

What's more, the *Financial Times* missed at least one other key force at work—growing economic insecurity. The Rockefeller Foundation reported that one in five Americans lost more than 25 percent of their household income in 2009. That was during the height of the economic crisis, but it wasn't unusual. Even before the crisis, a big loss of income routinely hit one in seven Americans in any given year. Economic insecurity adds insult to the injury of declining wages—Americans can barely count on the income that they do get.[2]

Against these forces, Americans have been falling back for years on longer hours, putting both spouses to work, and taking on ever-higher amounts of debt. These "coping mechanisms," as political economist Robert Reich calls them, appear to have finally maxed out.[3]

These trends are not new. But they have become more critical in the aftershocks of the recent economic crisis and recession.

The challenge of our age is to deal with the intersection of all of these forces at the same time. We urgently need a path to more jobs and higher wages for Americans in a world increasingly characterized by outsourcing, globalization, rapid technology change, and volatility among jobs, careers, and companies. Americans clearly sense forces at work beyond their control, and this is driving their anxiety about outsourcing, globalization, and the future of the American Dream.

In some ways this isn't entirely new. We've faced big periods of anxiety before. In his book *The Post-American World*, Fareed Zakaria notes that there have been four waves of fear in America's recent past. The first came with Sputnik when Russia suddenly looked set to dominate the world. The second was in the 1970s when the oil crisis and the war in Vietnam undermined American confidence and provoked fears that the Organization of the Petroleum Exporting Countries (OPEC) would buy up everything. After that came the Japanese challenge of the 1980s, along with an entire industry of pundits to explain how Japan would overtake America and dominate our economy.

Three times someone else has been about to rule the world. Three times the challenger has faded. Michael Crichton's *Rising Sun* was published at the peak of the hysteria—just as Japan was entering the start of its lost decade of economic stagnation (a lost decade that turned into two).

Today we are in the midst of a fourth wave of fear over the rise of China, the outflow of jobs, and a growing sense of economic stagnation and political decline, all amplified by the Great Recession and its aftermath. But the angst and the underlying problems outlined above have been building for much longer. To make sense of what is going on, it is important to place this latest challenge within a larger strategic context. Before we can rise to the occasion, we need to understand what is really happening because it's a lot bigger than one recession or even one decade.

Most commentators start by comparing today against the period between 1945 and the 1970s when the American economy delivered prosperity and stability in the form of a rock-solid middle class. This inevitably leads to a diagnosis on what has changed and who is to blame. The problem with this comparison and diagnosis is that they are based on a post-war period that is, to take liberties with Churchill, an anomaly encased in an aberration enshrouded by a conundrum. This period was so unique that it is unlikely to be repeated and even less likely to offer a guide for the future. Let's take a look at why that is so.

The anomaly—and it's a big one—is that the rest of the world was pulverized into wreckage at the close of World War II. It took thirty years for Europe and Japan to rebuild and begin competing across the full breadth of industries they once had. In that time, the US economy, middle class, and corporate multinationals enjoyed a near monopoly on industrial production and a free ride from real competition. These conditions will never be duplicated again without a corresponding global war from which we emerge nearly unscathed and everyone else is destroyed—an unappealing prospect, I hope.

The aberration is that the long period of Western ascendency over the rest of the world is finally coming to an end. We are reverting to the historical mean in which China, India, and large swaths of the rest of the world are full participants in the global economy. This is happening at a time when distance has become virtually meaningless, the world has grown flat. Some are calling this period the Great Convergence as the major developing countries rapidly catch up with the West. Hand wringing won't change the trend, nor is it desirable for the majority of the world to remain mired in poverty.

Finally, there is the conundrum of technology, which is advancing at an ever-faster rate, delivering huge productivity gains on the one hand and massive dislocation of workers on the other. This is Alvin Toffler's *Future Shock* in action.

Consider this: In 1905, 31 million Americans—more than one third of the population of 84 million—lived on farms. Today, less than 1 percent of the US population of 300 million lives on farms and fewer than 1 million Americans claim farming as a principal occupation. Yet we still produce one of the largest agricultural surpluses in the world while using virtually the same amount of land for farming. How is this possible? A big factor is the productivity of agricultural labor, which changed dramatically with the advent of mechanization—think: tractors. In 1890, it took one worker to farm 27.5 acres of farmland. By 1990, one worker could farm 740 acres, a massive increase by any measure.[4]

Manufacturing is following the same path. Many low-skill jobs may have gone overseas, but many higher skill manufacturing jobs are being consumed by technology and process improvement, consolidation, and automation. This transformation isn't driven by tractors, as in agriculture, but by computers and robotics. Across most product types, fewer and fewer workers are needed to operate a factory and maintain or increase production each year.

Here's a more tangible example: I have a friend who owns a small company that makes custom granite countertops. A decade ago, he would have employed dozens of workers to manufacture each new countertop by hand. Today, he owns one machine that is about the size of a shipping container. You punch in the precise specs of the countertop you want to create and load the granite slab. The machine does the rest, carving and milling away until it produces a perfect piece in record time. As a result, my friend's employees are mostly drivers and salespeople, not skilled craftsmen.

Despite these changes, we remain one of the largest manufacturing powers in the world. While China reportedly won the top spot in 2010, the US share of global manufacturing was roughly constant at 22 percent of global manufacturing output from 1980 all the way through 2008, despite a steady downward trend in total manufacturing employment during that time.[5]

Longing for the days when we had more manufacturing jobs fails to acknowledge a natural technical progression and business evolution that will slowly, inexorably mean we continue to produce more advanced manufactured goods with an ever smaller number of workers.

This trend does not stop with manufacturing. It is about to be unleashed in the services economy on a much larger scale. The *New York Times* has been running a catchy series of articles in 2010 and 2011 on advances in artificial intelligence and robotics.[6] There is the automated software that is learning to take our customer service calls. There are the robotic cars that Google has created that will one day drive themselves. There is the surrogate robot for remote workers. The list goes on and on. To cap it all off, IBM's Watson computer handily beat humans in a game of Jeopardy in February 2011, demonstrating that computing power and artificial intelligence were making big leaps forward.

In perusing these articles or watching Watson in action, it becomes clear that we will see more, not less, revolutionary leaps in technology and innovation across the breadth of our economy in the coming years. These breakthroughs will be disruptive—fortunes will be made, industries created. But on the opposite side of the ledger, obsolete industries will decay and die, and so will the jobs they currently support. People will be displaced and forced to find new jobs, even whole new careers. It will be a painful process of churn and change for individuals even if the aggregate employment numbers wind up looking okay.

I think of these as singularity tremors. The singularity is a cult-like idea among some technophiles that predicts an exponential increase in technology resulting in the eventual fusion of human and machine. Or something like that. I am not completely sure of a singularity but entirely certain that we will see a series of technology-driven breakthroughs that will cause job shocks throughout the economy. The forces of technological innovation are accelerating the process of change, including job and economic displacement, even as they bring new gadgets and ways of doing things.

This context—anomaly, aberration, conundrum—is the place to start looking at remedies. It is a waste of time to look backward at the post-war period and the rather simple formula that was successful then. The future will not look like the past. Like it or not, we are living in interesting times.

I could not write a book about outsourcing, a practice that contributes to these challenges, without also attempting to articulate a vision of how Americans can yet succeed and be more prosperous in this changing world and within the context of the challenges we face. But solving our challenges goes far beyond the issue of just outsourcing. It means helping all Americans be more prosperous, not just the subset that lose a job specifically because of outsourcing. As I've shown earlier, just 2 percent of job loss is from outsourcing in any given year. Yet the other 98 percent is equally painful to individuals and communities. I'm not trying to solve just the 2 percent problem. I'm going after the big picture. The proposals outlined in the following pages attempt to address this bigger picture.

While pessimists may look at our current challenges and dysfunctional politics and think we are 'screwed', I don't agree. I believe prosperity is possible for every American. I believe America can succeed. I think our kids can and will do well.

It is time for specifics.

CHAPTER 29

The 5 Percent Nation

OUR GOAL SHOULD BE to become a 5 percent nation. What I mean by this is an economy characterized by both 5 percent top-line economic growth in GDP as well as 5 percent growth in median family income. Both components are inexorably linked. The former without the latter is not a path that is fair, stable, or sustainable. Nor can the latter happen without the former.

Every politician wants growth, of course. But in partisan terms, it seems a lot like Republicans really only care about economic growth and Democrats mostly focus on ways to increase median family income. We need both to succeed.

Top-line economic growth is critical. Writing in *Time Magazine* in June 2011, Rana Foroohar compared the impact of different rates of growth. If the United States were to achieve 3.9 percent economic growth, our budget would start to balance, our debt would look more manageable, and we would argue less over pensions and entitlements. At only 2 percent economic growth for an extended period of time, we start to look like Greece, a country facing a swelling debt, deep political crisis, and major restructuring of pensions and entitlements, not to mention the protests in the streets and the risk to the European Union's very cohesion.[7]

At the same time, some of our biggest social ills are caused by income inequality and the practice of skewing benefits to the rich. That is why median wage growth, rather than just average wage growth, is so critical. While the average is everyone's income divided by the number of people, the median is a measure of the halfway point. In the context of income, it's the point at which half of the people make more and half make less. If we focus just on the average, the rich skew the numbers higher. Imagine

Warren Buffet walking into a bar. The average income in that bar just jumped through the roof. The median income barely budged.

Here's why growth is so important: Multinational companies talk a lot about Strategic Growth Markets, usually referring to developing countries like China, India, South Korea, and Indonesia. They also include countries in Eastern Europe and Latin America. All of these countries share a recent track record of rapid economic growth, young populations, and a future of economic dynamism. Every company wants a piece of that story.

America is not in that club anymore. We are a mature economy, which means our growth is sedate and expected to remain so. Our population is aging. Our economy is sputtering. Consumers are deleveraging. The most optimistic forecasts predict growth in the range of 2 to 3 percent far into the future, which is hardly sizzling. Countries, even large ones, with slow growth are places where companies make only modest investments. It's where they keep the lights on, not where they place their big bets.

We need to change that picture. I would like to see America viewed once again as a Strategic Growth Market, one that is growing rapidly and with clear prospects for more of the same. We are the biggest economy today. We need a path to more growth and dynamism in median income tomorrow. Rapid growth creates the space and opportunity for people to gain higher wages. It creates new opportunities and jobs for Americans at every level of society. It energizes companies into investing, building, and hiring. It will also generate growth and opportunity to replace the fear of globalization and outsourcing with optimism and confidence.

The Carnegie Endowment for International Peace recently forecast the US economy in 2050 would hit $38.6 trillion in constant 2005 US dollars. That forecast presumed annual average growth of 2.7 percent, which is fair but not impressive. In the same period, China is projected to grow at an average 5.6 percent annually, hitting a total size of over $45 trillion and eclipsing the United States as the world's largest economy by 2032 (some scenarios say before 2020) as surely as it eclipsed Japan as the second largest in 2010.[8]

I would argue that to be a more prosperous and dynamic America, to provide the room for increasing wages and benefits for all Americans, not just the rich, our goal should be a $50 trillion economy in constant dollars within forty years. That means more than tripling in size within a single generation, by 2050, as a strategic goal and developing the policies that will help get us there. Growth of this caliber would provide a path for more Americans to succeed and prosper, significantly increasing median income. This is the only antidote to stagnation, inequality, fear of outsourcing, and—the most pernicious of all—reduced expectations.

The question, of course, is how to make this happen.

The Big Ideas

An agenda to put America on a path to rapid economic growth and simultaneously to increase median income requires structural changes to our economy and politics and needs some mix of the following broad policy planks:

A New Educational Frontier
A New Social Contract
Growing America
Doubling Exports
A Green Revolution
A Zero Deficit
Strategic Growth Markets
The Final Frontier—An Exploration Economy
A New War on Poverty

These broad themes constitute components of an overall strategy for shifting from an indebted, declining American power with an embattled middle class to a more dynamic, fast-growing country whose brightest days truly are still ahead of it. I believe these are the themes that would transform America into a strategic growth market on a journey to reaching a $50 trillion economy by 2050 with a middle class that is increasingly prosperous.

CHAPTER 30

A New Educational Frontier

CREATING A FOUNDATION for growth and prosperity for American workers and companies requires fundamentally expanding access to education and dramatically up-skilling our workforce. Education is the single most important structural change we have to make in our economy. It is the foundation for greater productivity, faster growth, and better wages.

We will win or lose the future by how we meet this challenge. To do it well, we must revolutionize access to higher education and close the gaps in K–12 learning and achievement. We must simultaneously increase the velocity of educational attainment while dramatically lowering cost.

University of America

America once had the most educated workforce in history. Today, we are losing ground. A little over 40 percent of American adults aged twenty-five to sixty-four have completed a two-year degree or more. That is behind Russia, Japan, Canada, South Korea, and New Zealand, but it is still respectable.[9]

However, the picture is not so good for Americans in the twenty-five to thirty-four age bracket. While the rest of the world is rushing to educate their young, the United States is stuck in neutral. Over 55 percent of adults aged twenty-five to thirty-four in Canada, South Korea, and Russia now have at least an associate's degree. In the United States, the number is stuck at 40.4 percent. Among younger adults we are also behind Norway, Israel, France, Belgium and Australia.[10]

As the world shifts to a knowledge economy with a greater need for skilled, knowledgeable workers, the future prosperity of America as a whole rests on the ability to break down barriers to higher education and to dramatically increase America's throughput—in both absolute and relative numbers—attending, completing, and revisiting higher education throughout their life and career. As industries rise and fall, individual workers will need to re-skill and re-educate on an unprecedented scale. In its current form, our system does not make this feasible. We need to become a learning society in practice, not just in words.

Some studies suggest that we set a goal of 55 percent college attainment, seeking to match countries that have nearly reached that point today. As a goal, this is too modest. Other countries won't stand still, and by the time we have reached this benchmark, our competitors will be well past it. We still won't have gained the top slot, sparking yet another round of soul searching, analysis, and debilitating debate.

Yet that top slot is attainable. We can and should set out to achieve it decisively. Doing so requires setting the bar far above what our competition can envision or obtain and designing a system that can make it happen, one that is uniquely American. This requires revolutionizing access to higher education for all Americans, not just increasing the number of Pell Grants. Land-grant colleges were revolutionary in their day. It is time for a revolution appropriate to our time.

Our goal for higher education attainment should be 80 percent of all Americans to achieve a minimum of an associate's degree and 50 percent a bachelor's undergraduate degree. This goal is nothing less than up-skilling an entire society on an unprecedented scale, and it is premised on the belief that higher education should be open to all Americans who are willing to do the work of studying regardless of their means.

I propose a University of America that writes a new contract with all Americans interested in lifelong learning. The goal of the University of America is quite simple. For adult learners (over the age of twenty-two), we will cut the cost of obtaining a full four-year college degree by 75 percent and we will increase the number of students working their way toward a degree by 400 percent or more.

Creating this breakthrough will require re-architecting our system of higher education for adult learners via the following three steps:

1. Create a National Testing Infrastructure for Adult Learners

Access to testing for college credit is the first barrier to a college education that needs to be dramatically changed for adult learners. Today, we have several mechanisms for testing and granting college credit. High school students can take one of thirty Advanced Placement (AP) tests to get college credit. These tests are administered through high school teachers and AP coordinators at schools. The program is managed by a private nonprofit organization, the College Board. Adult learners can take advantage of the College Board's testing program called CLEP, or College Level Examination Program, which offers college credit for what people have learned on their own or through jobs.[11] This testing infrastructure is far too limited in scope, relevance, and accessibility.

I would propose the construction of a ubiquitous, national testing infrastructure focused on adult learners with tens of thousands of testing locations available at virtually every public institution, including libraries, K–12 schools, public colleges, community centers, and city halls. A facility does not have to be elaborate. It can be a roped off section of a library overseen by a reference librarian. It could be a room or alcove off the office of the local elementary school. Testing would use online tools but would be proctored on-site. Facilities would be open to the public throughout the day and into late evening for convenient access, and tests should be open to drop-in traffic, appointments optional.

Leveraging our existing public institutions should mean the cost of individual tests can be kept low—as little as $5 per test. We need to make it cheap, easy, and convenient to take a test for college credit on any day of the week, on demand, at a nearby location in every community in the nation.

The goal of an expanded national testing infrastructure will be to replace the handful of AP and CLEP tests with hundreds of nationally recognized standard tests whose acceptance is required by all colleges and universities in the United States that receive public funding. All American citizens and residents must be eligible to quickly and easily register for a test and begin accruing college credits at their own pace and on their own schedule, without ever being required to sit an SAT or to enroll in a specific college. Aptitude tests would be shelved for adult learners—results are what matter. I see this network serving tens of millions of adult Americans every year and perhaps a greater number of international adult learners.

Revenue generated through testing should be largely focused on increasing budgets for testing locations such that hours and access can be expanded.

2. Divide College Curriculums into Fact-Based vs. Context-Based Courses
A typical undergraduate curriculum includes a progression from basic survey courses to more specialized courses. Twenty years ago (or so), when I attended undergraduate classes, the typical 100-level introductory course was conducted in a large hall that could seat eight hundred or more students. Typically, a lively professor instructed and entertained the mammoth audience. However, there was no real interaction between the professor and the students. It was feasible then, and I suspect no less so now, to skip classes and study the book. Not only was the class content what I would describe as a mostly straightforward, fact-based review of material in the text, but it was split up over nine weeks with typically just three to five hours per week of class time. I would define courses like this as fact-based.

At the opposite end of the spectrum are the 400-level courses with fewer than twenty students, in which there is significant, meaningful interaction between professors and students. The focus is higher order concepts that require a great deal of explanation, much of it nuanced or sophisticated. These are heavily context-based courses.

Facts are objective. Context requires explanation and interaction.

It's true that a professor can enliven even the most basic, fact-based 100-level course. Today's system of higher education is structured on this precept. I would agree with (mostly) preserving this system for younger learners. For adult learners over the age of twenty-two, however, I believe the costs in time and money of this approach far outweigh the benefits and that as much as 75 percent of a typical undergraduate curriculum across virtually any discipline can and should be devolved into fact-based components.

People are capable of learning facts in many different ways. Class-based instruction is only one way. Once a curriculum is divided up and tests are created for the fact-based components *and* these tests can be taken independently of ever having to enroll in a given college or university, people will suddenly be free to learn independently through any means possible. Many of these might be cheap or even free.

Such means might include hitting the books and learning independently. Some people might prefer using online tools, blogs, or courseware provided by the private sector or social websites that are already gaining recognition—or perhaps have yet to be invented. Open standards will drive more open-source curriculum and free online textbooks. Some people might gravitate to old-fashioned local, neighborhood study groups—a reinvention of book clubs. I think of this latter option as going from 'bowling alone' to studying together. Some people might even use services that are outsourced and done remotely. Anything is possible—and will likely be tried—if the system is opened up. In effect, every community, every neighborhood—large or small— has the potential to become a college town.

A third and final piece is required to complete the vision.

3. Develop Intensive, Short-Term Residencies for Degree Completion
If we empower people to study and obtain credit via testing for the fact-based portion of a college curriculum independent of a given college or university, then human interaction in the form of a professor becomes even more critical to bring it all back together at the end. In my opinion, the first two elements of a University of America *only* work if they are completed by an intensive, full-time residency program of at least four weeks. Students that have completed all their fact-based prerequisites then apply to colleges and universities to complete an intensive residency in order to receive a degree in their chosen subject.

The role of the professor in this becomes both more crucial and more valuable than in our current system. A residency program of this type would entail full-time, daily contact between students and a single professor, perhaps augmented by others. I would consider this an almost Socratic type education where one professor focuses on bringing it all together for a small group of students, conducts group projects, drives active engagement with each student, and counsels students to achieve their highest potential mastery of a given subject area.

Because this format is dramatically more intensive than our current system, it should be possible for some professors to specialize in this type of role and to be paid handsomely for it. Institutions ought to be able to increase throughput of students and to earn higher revenues.

For students, the total cost of education compared to today should be a fraction of the standard four-year tuition, thus they ought to be able and willing to pay a premium for the residency period—perhaps twice the cost of a semester of credits today.

The economics of this would result in increased revenue for participating colleges and educations, higher salaries for professors that are capable of leading this type of education, and because the residency is the only portion that is expensive, students should be able to complete a degree program at a fraction of today's cost—though not necessarily any quicker or easier in terms of overall effort.

How It Would Work

What I have outlined is more than a twist on today's online education. It is involves a significant set of structural changes that devolves power from our colleges and universities to people and communities. It's best illustrated by the story of two mid-career fictional characters: Beth and Jane.

Beth decided to pursue a four-year college degree through what I'll call the University of the Mythical Bird (or UMB for short). It's an online college that offers a robust set of popular degrees and offers both classroom and online coursework. Advertisements are everywhere and are driven by a huge marketing budget. They convince a lot of people, including Beth, to sign up. She decides on a degree in psychology and needs 120 credits to graduate. Credits cost $570 plus an electronic fee of $95. Most of her courses are three credits. Beth takes some courses downtown on the UMB campus during the evenings after work. One semester she takes an online course that is connected to a professor, whom she can ask questions and submit work to. She graduates in five years with a degree that cost $72,200 to earn and accrues a student debt of slightly more than $30,000.

Jane takes a different path. When the new administration was elected it did a crash program to roll out the University of America infrastructure, and now that it is two years old, Jane is one of nearly 20 million Americans that have enrolled. She too opts to pursue a degree in psychology. She knows from the online guidelines what courses to take and how many elective credits to accumulate, and she has consulted a volunteer career counselor at her church to understand the right sequence to take them in and what to watch out for.

Some of the early 100-level courses are easy. These are the basic Psychology 101 and Sociology 101 core curriculum courses. There is a wiki site that had most of the content for each of these courses available for free download. For each course, Jane studies the material, prints out and takes a few practice tests, and when she thinks she is ready, takes the test for each of these courses at her local library. She passes her first three courses this way with scores above 90 percent and is excited to start accumulating credits that she can use at any college or university in the country. Her total cost so far is less than $100 for the testing and an extra book she bought to help her prep (and her time on the weekends and evenings spent studying).

One of the courses she needs is English Composition, or essay writing. Jane wants a more interactive experience with this course. A friend recommends a local women's study group that is forming up around this topic, so Jane joins and they met every Wednesday night for ten weeks to talk shop and practice writing and composing college-level essays. Two of the women in the group have already gone through this course and are coaching the others. They rotate houses for meetings, and the format is a potluck dinner where everyone can enjoy a glass of wine while they talk, practice writing, and review and critique each other's essays. By the end, they are doing practice essay tests, and Jane is getting pretty good. When it's time to take the test, everyone in the group goes the same weekend, submits their essays, and gets their scores back. Everyone passes—although not everyone scores the same—and the group has a party at Jane's house to celebrate.

Then she delves into some of her core psychology courses: General Psychology, History of Psychology, Human Psychology, Cognitive Psychology, and more. This is the process of building up a body of knowledge in psychology, and each course dives deep into a topic area. Jane uses some of the free sites on the web, hits YouTube for some free lectures, and attends an ongoing discussion group in her community that is led by two psychologists who like to help students learn the profession. Jane progresses over nearly a dozen courses in her core curriculum over the next two years, building a base of factual knowledge about the field of psychology.

Math and statistics are the courses Jane least looks forward to and is least confident about. She signs up at a local community college for two math courses so she can have a traditional instructor-led course. She does well and nails the tests. For statistics, she uses an online tutor from India. It is a little pricier than the community college course, but she wants the extra attention and support, although she can't afford a US-based tutor. Her Indian instructor, Rajiv, does a great job on their thrice weekly Skype calls, and soon Jane passes her statistics test too.

After four and a half years, Jane has accumulated enough credits and passed enough tests on her prerequisites that she is ready for the final sprint to a degree. She applies to the University of Washington for one of its four-week intensive programs, and she secures a slot four months out, when she can take paid leave from her employer.

Jane lives in Oregon, so commuting is out of the question. She chooses a residency option and moves into a dorm on the Seattle campus for those four weeks. Her professor is Jim Clarke. Her group includes nineteen other students, and for $7,000 each, they go through an intensive program of six to eight hours of class and experiential learning a day, all guided by Jim. (It is a good deal for the university, of course. Less living costs, the class contributes nearly $80,000 in total tuition revenue to the university and Jim runs six to eight courses a year, which means $480,000 to $640,000 in tuition revenue for one teacher in one year. The university can afford to pay Jim a good salary and Jim spends his time between classes and clinical research.)

Evenings and weekends are almost entirely filled with homework that involves both individual and small group projects, written papers, and presentations. There are lab and observation sessions, role playing, and case studies. Jane realizes that when the university brochures described the residency as intense, they meant it. Her group is diverse, and there are a few tensions and tears along the way. One student quits and goes home, but everyone else sticks it out. By the end, the remaining students pass and receive a bachelor's degree from the University of Washington, and Jane has made some new friends from places as varied as Texas and Kuala Lumpur. Jane leaves proud of her new degree, her new friends, and with some new ambitions.

The total cost of her degree is about $9,000 over the five years it took her to work her way through the credits and complete the final intensive program to obtain her degree. Her student debt for all this is roughly $3,000.

Along the way, she also became part of a new community of active learners in her town. With a first degree under her belt, she is already thinking about what her next degree in five or ten years will be. There are so many possibilities.

Summary

With a University of America, I believe we can increase the level of college participation and degree attainment across our society to 80 percent within ten years and that this would have a significant impact on our country's potential for productivity, economic growth, and competitiveness. In this model, the vast majority of Americans are able to get a college degree and the new metric for countries to compete on becomes the percentage with advanced degrees or more than one undergraduate degree.

For you as a reader, it would mean the chance to start accumulating college credits through virtually any means that will work for you—at a fraction of the cost of today's tuition. These credits would be recognized at any publicly funded college or university.

As a nation, a University of America would dramatically alter the velocity and attainment of higher education in America and provide a new and compelling competitive edge. It would devolve power to earn college credit from the institutional level today to a broad and diverse set of social learning groups backed by a national testing infrastructure. In effect, every community could become a college town by promoting learning as a new social and group activity.

A New Frontier for K–12

The challenges faced by America's public K–12 education have been highlighted in stark terms over the past few years. Here are a few facts:

Up to one third of the country's most experienced teachers will retire over the next four to five years at the same time that new teacher job attrition will result in the loss of an additional one third.[12] Meanwhile, the graduation gap between suburban and urban schools is nearly 20 percent according to the America's Promise Alliance, a nonprofit focusing on improving the nation's dropout rate. The outcome of failing city schools is a massive waste of talent heavily skewed against minority populations, and that has a lifelong impact on earnings potential.[13] Finally, the economic cost of this achievement gap has been quantified by McKinsey, and the number is stunning. Collectively America is losing between $1.3 and $2.3 trillion *every year* in economic activity, 9 to 16 percent of GDP, by not having successfully closed the achievement gap and educating kids to their potential. McKinsey characterizes this as a permanent depression in economic activity.[14] The inescapable conclusion is this: We are losing ground and it is costing us a fortune.

Primary education is a key requirement for both individuals and countries to remain competitive. There is no shortage of initiatives, ideas, reforms, and fads on how to improve K-12 education. They include, but are not limited to, charter schools, teacher accountability, teacher training, use of technology, big investments in mega-expensive schools, Teach for America, more pay (even six-figure teacher salaries), and longer hours.

All these initiatives have their place and role, but I don't think they are enough to get us to where we need to be. Certainly reform in the shape of accountability and performance measures as well as rewards inspired by the Obama Administration's Race to the Top challenge have their part—as does teacher training—but these seem to be the minimum requirements that we should already have in place.

Teach for America brings talented and dedicated people into the education field, and this also makes an important contribution. Yet they are a small number within the total pool of millions of teachers, and most of these talented people do their required two-year service and then move back to higher paying careers.

Charter schools are not performing any better, and in some cases are worse, than their public alternatives according to a recent study by Stanford.[15] While they have a place, such data suggests that the fervor and focus on charter schools seems very much a faith-based initiative.

Throwing money at schools and higher teacher salaries has its virtues, but this action is fiscally unsustainable and may not produce better results. Longer school days and more days in the school year would make a huge difference, but these schedules are unlikely to change as long as teacher unions retain any influence and budgets remain locked into the same structural math. All these efforts are worth pursuing on their own merits, but they don't change the overall game.

When I look for inspiration about what to do, I find myself dwelling on two things. First, from what I have read, elite prep schools have a teacher-student ratio of 1:8 and sometimes lower. The best prep schools in our country effectively send all their graduates on to prestigious four-year universities by applying an overwhelming level of staff, attention, and focus to their students. It doesn't hurt that these kids come from advantaged backgrounds with families that are most often highly educated themselves. By contrast, most public schools have a stated teacher-student ratio in the upper teens, and in the classroom it is actually much higher. In Oregon, some high school math classes now have more than forty students per teacher. The concept of personal attention in such a class size is a joke.

The second inspiration is based on personal experience. I have two children, the oldest of which attends our local elementary school. Over the last several years, I've learned what a high-performing school actually looks like. First, it has a great principal willing to experiment. Second, it has exceptional teachers at every level who have experience and are effective with the students. But that isn't enough. It also has an extremely committed parent community that volunteers time at the school, is fully engaged in the classroom, and runs fundraisers nearly constantly. As the old adage says, it really does take a village. The result is test scores that are consistently outstanding.

But there are two caveats. This high-performing school could still be better. And it helps that this particular village is fairly prosperous, highly educated, and has the time and desire to truly engage with the school. In a poorer, more urban area, it is hard to see how this dynamic can be matched without outside help. The problems are bigger, the resources thinner, the parents more stretched and with less time to contribute.

The problems we have to solve are how to give every student the level of attention—on par with an elite prep school—that they need to excel and how to provide a rich network of support within schools at a price we can afford. Teachers are neither the entire problem nor the entire solution. A Lake Wobegon desire for every teacher to be above average is not possible statistically, economically, or politically, although it is what every parent (and taxpayer) wants.

To solve this dilemma, I propose a National Teacher Assistant Voucher program to fund 5 million part-time teaching assistants for our nation's schools.

Here are the basic parameters for how it would work:

- Teaching assistants would be paid $10/hour for twenty hours per week for nine months. I estimate the cost of this for 5 million teaching assistants to be in the range of $35 to $40 billion.
- The program would be focused entirely on retiring baby boomers, and the cash transfers would be intended to supplement Social Security benefits.
- The stipend payments would be tax-free.
- Vouchers would be heavily skewed toward underperforming schools and underperforming classrooms within schools, identified by student achievement scores and metrics.
- Teaching assistants would work closely with a lead, full-time teacher in a team effort that divides students into smaller groups in order to achieve maximum attention for each pupil. The ratio of teacher-plus-assistants to students could be as low as 1:4 in underperforming classes.
- The program would be complemented by a requirement for aggressive truancy enforcement.

I believe that children have an enormous capability to overcome any obstacle if they are given enough time, attention, and training to succeed. I believe this program is the only way to achieve these results at the scale necessary to solve the problem.

It is a cost-effective solution and comes at a fraction of the price of attempting a big salary increase for teachers across the nation, a bill that would run to several hundred billion dollars at a time when hard budgetary choices are being debated.

If McKinsey's estimate of what we are losing every year ($1.3 to $2.3 trillion annually) in economic activity because of an under-educated workforce is correct, then here's the simple business case: over ten years, we spend $400 billion to earn $10 to $20 trillion in additional national income. There is no business person I have ever met that would not sign off on those numbers. This program puts more people in the classroom, and its results would be immediate.

A National Teacher Assistant Voucher program also provides baby boomers with supplemental income to bolster low retirement savings and potentially lower Social Security payments, an honorable and fair trade that allows retirees to compensate for their failure to save during their work years and also trades on their accumulated skills and knowledge, all wrapped in a mission of community service. Make no mistake. We need to offer a means of earning income (preferably in return for a valuable community service) to this large voting block of citizens before they demand it in some other form via the ballot box anyway. I would prefer to offer it as a fee for service rather than an entitlement handout.

This program would immediately invest in closing the achievement gap in our K–12 educational system, which is undermining the American Dream of social mobility and opportunity for many of our own citizens, while it also denies our economy the potential to grow faster by creating too few skilled employees.

Summary

I believe these two initiatives—a University of America and a National Teacher Assistant Voucher program—would truly put us on the leading edge of a new educational frontier and that the payoff for America would be a better educated workforce, higher paying jobs that drive a significant jump in median income, productivity growth, and a better potential for economic growth for the next generation.

CHAPTER 31

A New Social Contract

THE OLD SOCIAL contract is dead. We need a new one.

In the post-war paradigm, companies were built to last. They promised their employees job stability and ever-increasing wages, and, in exchange for a lifetime of work, a defined pension. Those times are gone. Today's world is ferociously competitive, and few companies are going to be around for the full expanse of anyone's career. Most will collapse, sell out, break up, consolidate, or slowly dwindle away. And this will happen at a faster rate than ever before. This is the big picture.

At a personal level, this shows up as economic insecurity. As companies restructure, reinvent, and fail, people are going to lose jobs and income more often throughout their working career than even our current turbulent times suggest. This is not a huge problem for the young. They have time to adapt and have less to lose. It is a disaster for mid-career professionals.

The problem is that losing a job has become a personal and financial catastrophe for many Americans, especially those in the middle class who have families and are financially stretched. Americans are exposed and vulnerable to an unprecedented period of change at home and abroad. The result is that we are in danger of acculturating a sense of fear about competing in the world—and shaping our politics and economy accordingly.

If we want to maintain or expand our open system and its openness to trade and globalization (not to mention our humanity), then we need to address the underlying and very real fears that Americans have about losing their jobs. We have to make the consequences of losing a job less catastrophic and painful. We need to protect workers, not jobs. We need to do this while avoiding the moral hazard of rewarding people for not working and without building an overarching welfare state.

Here are a couple of ideas:

Wage Insurance

The Council on Foreign Relations (CFR) has found that middle-aged, middle-class workers who have been on the job twenty years or more typically lose in excess of 30 percent of their income in their next job. A forty-year-old worker who loses just 25 percent of her income in her next job and works for twenty years would have had a total lifelong wage loss of $160,000, the current price of a house in most places in the United States.[16] This is the high price of starting over. A program of wage insurance that focuses on long-tenured workers would address one of the biggest underlying fears that Americans face in our increasingly dynamic economy—the impact of a lifelong drop in earnings as a result of losing a job.

CFR recommends a robust program of wage insurance based on length of tenure that would replace 50 percent of lost wages, last four years or more, set the income level much higher than today's $50,000 income cap and maximum of $10,000 in annual benefits, and include a deductible (e.g., a worker would not qualify unless income loss is greater than 5 percent). If carefully crafted, a broad program of wage insurance could avoid the moral hazards of paying people not to work and would help encourage people to move into new jobs faster, even when the new job pays less than the last one. It would significantly reduce the risk of people losing homes and breaking up families over financial difficulties.

Such a program would insure workers against large, permanent financial losses. CFR estimates the cost in the range of $3 to $4 billion annually. It could be financed with a $2 to $3 monthly insurance premium from each worker. It could also be financed by extending the waiting period for today's unemployment insurance. This would mean people have to, in effect, self-insure for short periods of unemployment with their own savings. Some combination of both approaches seems reasonable, and both rely on people paying their way and saving more rather than putting a heavier burden on a strapped federal budget.

Personally, I would be not only willing but ecstatic to pay $3 each month (even $20) to insure myself against a dramatic, catastrophic loss in wages from a layoff. An effective wage insurance program is a critical first step to help all hard-working middle-class American workers reduce the worst consequences of losing a job.

Universal Health Care

Despite the Obama Administration's best intentions, health care remains unfinished business in my mind, and it is also a key part of the social contract with American workers. With the recent health care reform, we got much closer to universal coverage and protecting workers against losing health care when they lose a job. The insurance industry's practice of recision—canceling people's insurance on a technicality for any pretext possible—is finished. Discrimination against preexisting conditions will end. These are all positive result. But we didn't get to universal coverage and, most importantly, we didn't reduce costs.

A study by McKinsey Global Institute, prior to health care reforms, found that the United States spends nearly 25 percent more than it should when adjusted against benchmarks of other countries and for level of wealth. The overspending includes $66 billion in higher drug costs, $75 billion in profits and taxes that would not be incurred in a public system, and $98 billion in extra administrative expenses (including sales and marketing). All told, McKinsey estimates the United States spends over $477 billion more than it should based on the size and wealth of our economy compared to other advanced economies.[17] Countries in Europe with socialized medicine spend a little over half of what we do in terms of the size of their economy. We spend nearly 18 percent of GDP. The average across other industrialized countries is closer to 9 percent.

If socialized medicine means I get better service at a lower cost and we as a country could save $500 billion a year and possibly much more, then I'm all for it. I care more about what works and its impact on the bottom line than I do about anyone's rigid ideological definitions. I want a lower total cost of ownership, and I want that money returned to families and businesses around the country.

I don't want a single-payer system run entirely by government. I'm just conservative enough to be afraid of government bureaucracy, but private industry has not proven they can deliver operational efficiency and lower costs compared to alternatives widely available in other advanced economies.

We would be better served by a system of competing nonprofits that are strictly regulated by government and with common standards that allow for greatly reduced administrative expenses, transparent pricing, and shareable electronic health records. We should seek to implement a system closer to the French or German models. Transitioning to such a system would free up savings for increased economic activity by businesses and consumers.

Universal health care that lowers the overall total cost of ownership for America would increase economic growth more sustainably than a tax break because it translates directly to increasing family income and lowering business expenses, and it is fiscally sustainable and lowers long-term entitlement spending. Containing health care costs is one of the most important steps in ending wage stagnation in America. Not only is it better for the economy, it would be better for all Americans who could stop living in fear of losing their coverage or getting charged an arm and a leg for it.

Summary

To prepare and sustain American workers in an era of global transformation, we need to increase their resilience, their ability to recover from a temporary setback, whether that is a job loss or an illness. As a nation we need to be braver in the face of global competition that will only increase.

We need a strategic framework, a new social contract, for American citizens to be resilient in the face of economic catastrophe at the community and individual level. We need American workers to face up to the potent and unprecedented mix of global competition, rapid technology change, and economic churn knowing that we have their back.

I believe the key elements of this are wage insurance and universal health care. With these protections in place, American workers can stop being afraid to compete globally.

CHAPTER 32

Growing America

IMMIGRATION IS an American core competency.

I know that must seem strange to read against the backdrop of recent controversies in Arizona and when some politicians are challenging the Fourteenth Amendment. But it is true.

We are a nation built on immigration. Some of our most important icons (the Statue of Liberty) and national imagery (the melting pot) center on immigration. Those who are vociferously lambasting immigrants today are almost entirely of immigrant stock themselves. The only difference is how many generations have passed in this country and what the country of origin is.

We regularly naturalize over 1 million new citizens every year and have for some time. Their children have long provided the bulk of the additional population growth that underpins our economy and its growth and dynamism. In this sense, immigration is an important factor input that helps drive economic growth—immigrants purchase everything from food to clothing, services to houses.

Despite our flaws and controversies, we are more effective and more tolerant than Europe, Japan, or any other country at assimilating and making room for people from any nation or creed to participate in American life. And we get a lot back from it. We are richer economically, culturally, and politically for this ability to attract, welcome, and integrate immigrants.

But this isn't just about feeling good or being self-congratulatory. It's about cold, hard national strength and economic power. Immigration underpins American economic and military strength. It adds dynamism to our economy. It is the antidote to a future of fiscal crisis and anemic economic growth. It is the difference between an aging, declining superpower and the leader of the free world for the rest of this century and beyond.

It's time to open our doors wide.

Most population projections show America with a population of 310 million in 2010 growing to 438 million by the year 2050. This assumes not much change in the rate of immigration into this country over the next forty years. Immigration, in this scenario, would add 117 million people—the vast bulk of population growth and a significant component of economic growth—including people who immigrate and the children they will have while in America.[18]

At a relatively modest rate of 2.7 percent annual economic growth, an American economy of 438 million people grows to about $38 trillion by 2050. As noted earlier, that puts us in clear second place to China, which is forecasted to grow at 5.6 percent on average over the next forty years and reach an economy of over $45 trillion.[19] Our economic power and political clout will be greatly diminished in comparison. Meanwhile our population will have a dependency ratio of 72 (72 children and seniors for every 100 working Americans) compared to 59 today. We will be a country with an aging population, serious fiscal challenges, and a more economically and politically powerful competitor (China) that will challenge us at every turn.

It doesn't have to be this way, and immigration is a key strategic opportunity and the most practical means to grow above our current economic trend potential. The Pew Charitable Trusts have calculated that if we increased our immigration rate over the next forty years starting at around 1.5 million and growing from there over the full 40 years, our population would be 496 million by 2050. I estimate that our economy could be $5 to $10 trillion larger based on immigration's impact alone. That would put us closer to the $40 to $45 trillion range already. Our dependency ratio would drop to 69, a modest, but important change. In the process, we would partially ameliorate our looming fiscal crises and aging population. That's Pew's high-case scenario. If we can exceed our previous high-water marks for immigration and accept even more people, we will handily exceed the 2.7 percent annual growth forecast and become a much stronger economy and nation.

I would argue that we should work to better the Pew high-case scenario and shoot for a total population in the range of 500 to 550 million by 2050. We are a large country. We have the space. We can provide the opportunity. There is no shortage of people around the world that would like to have their shot at the American Dream. They work hard and contribute a lot when they get here. Immigrants are not lazy; they are dynamic risk takers. The factor input of immigration on a larger scale—sooner rather than later—would decisively change the future size, strength, and dynamism of America's economy.

Increasing immigration would not be without controversy. There would be challenges. We would need to expand our programs and policies on everything from jobs to education to help immigrants assimilate and get started in a new country. We would need to move more of the current adult American population up the skill ladder to make room for immigrant workers at every level, especially in the construction and building trades.

We would have to confront bigotry head-on. Bigotry and intolerance have accompanied every great wave of immigration from every new group into America whether it has been the Chinese or the Irish. My grandfather used to tell me the jokes he was subjected to as a young man (How many Irish does it take to screw in a light bulb?). Today's bigotry against Hispanics is just the latest outburst, focused on the largest, newest group. We will need to do better at confronting the vocal minority behind such bigotry as well as addressing the underlying worries about jobs and security within the broader public.

Despite the challenges, my vote would be to return to bedrock American values and open the door wide to much higher levels of legal immigration at every skill and education level from top to bottom. For purely economic reasons, I would put illegal aliens immediately on a path to legal citizenship and inclusion—and paying taxes. I would grant a green card to every foreign student that graduates from an American university with a bachelor's degree or more. I would grant green cards to H1B visa–holding, skilled workers after just twenty-four months of cumulative US work experience, encouraging them to settle down and stay permanently instead of taking their skills and knowledge back home. I would step up the volume of immigration from every geographic region and from every socioeconomic level.

America has the potential to attract ambitious, talented, and hard-working people willing to leave everything behind to start over in America, and if we tap this potential, we can grow our country at a scale necessary to reduce many of our largest challenges. We should seize this opportunity to change our future.

CHAPTER 33

Doubling Exports

THE PROBLEM WITH taking a long time to write a book is that you leave an opening for politicians to beat you to the punch on your best ideas. One of mine was doubling exports. President Obama got there first, and I applaud his boldness. But the devil is in the details, and the president left drafting up the details to a committee.

The problem is that committees live by compromise, not innovation. They will likely reiterate the common policy suggestions of exchange rate reform (meaning push China to appreciate its currency), more trade agreements, better export promotion and funding, investment in the infrastructure needed to compete, and smarter subsidies and support— the same game the Chinese are playing so well—to level the playing field. All of this makes sense, and these policies will help at a macro level. But I believe we have to do more to unleash what I call the animal spirits of how we compete overseas. We need to get American businesspeople truly amped up for a competitive fight far from home in foreign markets.

Today, America's share of exports is in the range of 12 percent of our economy. Yet many of our developed-country competitors have a much higher share of exports within their economy. Germany's is almost 50 percent, making it the global leader. The United Kingdom's share is 34 percent. France's is 30 percent. Japan's is 19 percent.[20] These are all respectable numbers. Although to be fair, it's easy to be international in Europe, where driving a couple of hours puts you in another country. In the United States, a six-hour flight is still within borders.

America has approximately 250,000 firms that engage in exports. That sounds like a big number, but it represents less than 1 percent of US firms with a payroll. Of the US firms that do export, the majority export to only one country (usually Canada). The biggest share of exports comes from large multinationals with internationalized supply chains and a diverse portfolio of foreign holdings and companies.

Fareed Zakaria has suggested that because the American market is so large, Americans have traditionally not tried to understand other markets and cultures.[21] We need to help them bridge that knowledge gap. We need to focus on the small- and medium-sized companies that have great products to sell but little presence and experience overseas.

To export, American firms have to be willing to try global trade, they have to understand how to do it (how to complete the paperwork, get paid, etc.), they need exposure to other markets (go there, see the opportunities), and they have to develop relationships with partners and customers in other countries. This means time on the ground. This is not an executive fly-by that involves staying in a nice hotel, taking a few meetings, and heading home. Too many American executives mistake this type of activity for gaining deep knowledge of local markets.

The good news is that these are all very practical problems. The skills needed to engage in a new market can be learned. Here's how to do it:

Boots on the Ground

For companies trying to sell overseas, the first line of engagement is the US Commercial Service. The Commercial Service has offices in one hundred cities in the United States and eighty countries worldwide. They are in effect our boots on the ground to help American business engage in global trade. They offer a range of services mostly to small- and medium-sized companies that are trying to break into overseas markets. They find partners, host visitors, and generate leads. They help get the ball rolling.

These are our foot soldiers in trade, and we need more of them. Many more. Today there are about 1,500 Commercial Service staff in both US and overseas offices. In China, the Commercial Service has a staff of a little over one hundred in six primary offices. This sounds like a lot, but China has fifty-eight cities that each have a population of more than 1 million people. According to McKinsey, by 2030, it will have 221 cities with a million or more people. Our Commercial Service in China is underfunded and understaffed, and this same scenario is likely true in virtually every other country as well. At a minimum, we need five hundred Commercial Service officers in China within four years. We probably need a similar number in India in the same time span, and in Brazil not long after that.

We should double the Commercial Service within two years and double it again two years after that. Virtually every city in the fastest-growing developing countries with a population of more than a million should have a Commercial Service office and a staff acting as the single point of contact for everything export related across the government.

Export Fellowships

The Commercial Service can help business find opportunities in international markets, but long-term success in a foreign market is largely built on firsthand knowledge of these markets. This knowledge includes insights about what customers want and how they buy as well as building strong relationships with local partners and distributors.

The vast swath of the American business community, especially small- and medium-sized businesses and manufacturers do not have much knowledge of places like China, India, Brazil, or Eastern Europe, or even France, the United Kingdom, or Germany.

To build these skills among our business community, I take a page from my experience as Peace Corps volunteer. If you really want to understand a local culture and identify opportunities, then you need to live for a period of time in that community and to meet people, learn customs, and build friendships. This is the raw material of experience and connections that will lead to business insights, opportunity, and success. The Peace Corps has tours that last two years. Businesspeople don't have that much time, but something on the order of three to six months should be required.

I propose that we complement a greatly expanded Commercial Service with an Export Fellowship program that subsidizes having US businesspeople work for three-month or six-month stints as adjuncts to Commercial Service offices overseas. While there, they would take basic language and cultural training, develop local business contacts, and identify opportunities for their companies to grow and sell. They would help the Commercial Service staff with ongoing work in support of other clients. The goal would be to complete the tour with a deeper understanding of local markets, opportunities, and to return home armed with business relationships for the long term.

The program could have qualifying criteria, such as limiting it to companies that don't currently have an office or sales over $1 million in the local market (that would eliminate any large, multinational corporations). Another requirement might be that the company CEO and senior staff commit to one or two visits during the employees' fellowship. This would guarantee the commitment of the company as a whole.

I believe this program should attempt to cycle 2,000 to 3,000 American businesspeople through Export Fellowships in its early years, ramping up to 10,000 to 12,000 per year as soon as possible.

Summary

Americans already derive many benefits from trade. Yet we are hammered by constant media images about trade deficits and jobs lost to foreign competition or outsourcing. We need to turn this tide of media images and change the game.

The good news is that there is a historic, global shift underway with markets in places like China, India, Brazil, Russia, and the Middle East becoming truly enormous. There are huge opportunities for American companies to export and to create jobs in America. If we can create a strategy to dramatically increase American companies' engagement in foreign markets, then Americans will feel more confident about their own prospects as well as the fairness of international trade.

We cannot rely on the old paradigm of pushing for fair exchange rates or opening markets if our businesses aren't willing to go overseas and engage with their markets. Japan's exchange rate has gone from 250 yen to the dollar in 1985 when the Plaza Accords were signed to the mid-seventies as recently as the winter of 2012. We have had a trade deficit almost the entire time. Focusing on exchange rates is not enough.

The answer is to engage and inspire American businesspeople to spend time on the ground with our Commercial Service men and women in countries like China, India, and Brazil and to help them gain the experience, insights, and contacts necessary to truly ramp up America's exports.

CHAPTER 34
_____

A Green Revolution

THERE ARE TWO NUMBERS that should matter to everyone regardless of their personal position on the science of global warming: $36 trillion and 40 million. The first is reportedly the investment that will be needed in the global economy to maintain oil and gas production at a high enough level to meet the expected demand over the next twenty to thirty years. The second is reportedly the number of jobs in green technology that will be created by 2050. The two numbers hint at the massive amounts of investment and jobs related to the intersection of energy and green technology.

Efforts to reduce carbon emissions within the global economy are likely to gain momentum over the next ten years. The countries and companies that lead this transformation will be at the forefront of creating jobs, industries, and economic growth well into the future. The ones that drag their feet will miss out on jobs and face a loss of competitiveness in these new technologies. (China, for instance, has already seized the lead in key industries from wind turbines to solar cell production while the United States dawdles.)

I believe America needs an aggressive strategy for going green to create the jobs and opportunities of the future. A grand strategy for reducing carbon would stop $400 to $700 billion a year from flowing out of our country for imported oil (to dictators and regimes that don't like us), would result in millions of jobs being created all across America, and would seize the moral and political high ground of saving the planet.

As much as I like this idea, there's a problem with the vision. When it comes to the environment, we have gotten ourselves locked into a zero-sum ideological struggle between the left and the right. The result is gridlock, and a failure to act that will deprive our country of the chance to lead the emergence of new industries and create the jobs of the future.

The emphasis on transforming our economy today to be more green is right in my mind, but it is not so in every American's. We are a divided nation on this topic. What we need is a way to give people choices and to let individuals decide for themselves so that neither the left nor the right is imposing their will on those who do not agree. We need to do this in a way that makes markets more efficient and that continues to build and shape America's future competitiveness in green technologies. I believe carbon labeling is a key means to bridge the divide.

Carbon Labeling

Today, consumers have no information about what carbon emissions are created in the process of making the products they purchase. That means that consumers who care about the environment have no way to make informed decisions or reward companies that are more environmentally sustainable.

The result: markets today are not operating efficiently and companies are not receiving the demand signals that can help them differentiate and respond to the market. Until consumers have this information and can use it in their purchasing decisions, industries are operating under faulty assumptions and allocating resources incorrectly. We need market-based signals so that consumers can vote with their wallet on what they value most. A carbon label would help achieve this.

The concept of carbon labeling is not new. The Carbon Trust in the United Kingdom has been working to develop a standard for years, and they are not the only ones. But adoption and consumer awareness are very low to date. Carbon labeling needs a breakthrough as quickly as possible so that consumers can begin exercising their vote on supply chains and economic activities. Consumer purchases should be the tail that wags the supply chain dog and that, in turn, will have an influence on government decisions—for better or worse—about energy infrastructure and investments.

I believe we should give consumers the information to decide for themselves. In the process we can make markets more efficient and help companies serve consumers more effectively, making a meaningful contribution to the environment in the process.

CHAPTER 35

A Zero Deficit

AMERICA NEEDS TO take responsibility for one of the biggest problems in the global economy: our role as a deficit country addicted to savings and financing from other nations. It is not sustainable, and it will lead to disaster at home and abroad. A nation addicted to debt and consumption is one that is destroying its own future and robbing from its children. A lack of stewardship is the kindest way to put it. It is time to do our part to rebalance the global economy by balancing our budget at home.

There are real-world consequences from our inability to balance our budget, and they extend beyond the growing burden to future generations. Alan Greenspan has suggested that fear and uncertainty about our public debt is causing the private sector to hold back on investing.[22]

Furthermore, our geopolitical power is diminishing by the month as we look increasingly enfeebled by our inability to reign in our profligacy. We look foolish and weak when we lecture China on exchange rates and their surpluses when we haven't the will to balance our budget and eliminate our need to run deficits—and when we depend on their money.

But perhaps most serious of all, we have acculturated a sense that we cannot solve our own problems, that our government and our political system are ineffective. This is causing a deep corrosion in Americans' public confidence. It is a malaise that undermines faith in democracy at home and abroad. Balancing our budget to end deficit spending is a critical step in rebuilding economic confidence, geopolitical power, and American pride.

In November 2010, Erskine Bowles and Alan Simpson, the co-chairs of President Obama's bipartisan commission to reduce the federal debt, released a starting point set of recommendations that catalyzed this debate. Their paper was soon followed by competing approaches from the Bipartisan Policy Center and others. In early 2011, Republicans introduced the Ryan Plan. Shortly after, President Obama offered his own solution to our fiscal mess.

The debate has started, and that is a healthy sign. In the summer of 2011, however, the debate turned fractious and messy and culminated in a debt ceiling deal that pleased no one and witnessed the United States being downgraded from its once iron-clad AAA rating. The follow-on debates will occur after this book goes to press. However, policymakers have several roadmaps, and there is no shortage of options for cutting the federal debt. The only missing ingredients are willpower and willingness to compromise—no small things in a divided Congress that is significantly polarized.

Still, there is hope—both for ourselves and for our children—that we will come to grips with our problems and reset America's fiscal trajectory onto a safer path. For my own part, the options for balancing our budget are many, so I would use the following principles to evaluate which mix of policies to follow:

- *Compromise:* A viable plan to reduce the debt will require a mix of tax increases and spending cuts. It cannot be just one or the other, and we will have to find a compromise between the parties about the right balance between the two—or elect a new Congress that can do the job.

- *Fairness:* Tax increases for the wealthy have to be on the table. Historically, when we as a nation have faced major crises, we increased our tax rates. During the Great Depression, the top tax rate was 79 percent. World War II brought it to 94 percent, and it remained high at 91 percent from the end of World War II until 1964 when it dropped to 70 percent. The top rate didn't come down to 50 percent until Reagan's first term in 1982. At a current maximum rate of 35 percent, we have some room to tinker with. Higher taxes on the wealthy seem reasonable and fair.

- *Shared Sacrifice:* I also believe every one of us should do our part to balance the budget, not just the wealthy. That includes reconsidering everything from entitlements to treasured deductions and making modest, phased, and appropriate changes—enough to balance our budget, but not enough to cater to the ideological extremes of either party.

- *Target Zero:* I believe we need to balance our budget, not target some so-called sustainable level of deficits. The target should be zero or a positive number including interest payments. We need an end to the culture of debt, as we did at the end of the 1990s. We have to begin rolling back total debt and targeting a surplus. Ultra-low interest rates will not last forever. We can only be strong if we can pay down or stop accruing debt, not simply grow it at a slower rate.

- *Corporate Taxes:* I would vote for lower corporate rates to boost our competitiveness, but I would also end all loopholes with the exception of investment in research and development, and physical plant and equipment in the United States.

- *Consumption and Energy Taxes:* Taxation can be used wisely to reinforce our strategic goals as a nation for the long term. We need to encourage less consumption and more exports. A consumption tax—rebated for exports—would help achieve both these goals and would add to the policy tools for promoting exports. An energy or gasoline tax that ratchets up over time would raise funds for needed infrastructure and clean tech investments, and it would send clear market signals to consumers on what to expect in the future.

- *Timing:* We have just lived through a near miss on a replay of the Great Depression. The economy is still vulnerable. It is picking up in 2012, but we are not out of the woods yet. We ignore the lessons of history about tightening too soon at our peril. We may not yet be able to call a hard stop on deficits while the economy is still recovering, but we need to begin chipping away at it now and charting a path to a full-fledged surplus by 2015 (including interest expense).

These are the basic principles that I personally will be using to evaluate how well Congress deals with our growing federal debt and ongoing deficits.

The recent rash of commissions and reports show that there is a mix of options for reducing our deficits and getting to a balanced budget. It is possible to solve this problem. Leadership and compromise are what is needed and I am personally still looking for the grand bargain.

We will face great challenges and great opportunities in the future. If we are a bankrupt nation or indebted to foreign powers, we will not have the freedom or ability to budget for any of these. We will be a hollow superpower, a paper tiger dismissed around the world. Balancing our budget by reining in our annual deficits and paying down our debt are the key steps to being a strong, thriving America with a prosperous economy in the future.

CHAPTER 36
_____

Strategic Growth Markets

EVEN AS WE REIN in our ballooning deficits and chart a path to a lower debt, we are faced with challenges that we cannot avoid. We must still invest in our economy in a way that meets competitive challenges from abroad and positions us for prosperity in the future. This means infrastructure, education, and science.

When it comes to infrastructure, we will have to face up to a simple reality: if you don't build things, you not only lose out on the economic growth and greater productivity that top quality infrastructure creates, but you also lose the skills to build and you miss out on all the practical insights and engineering breakthroughs that come from solving problems. This means you miss out on an entire ecosystem of products, services, and knowledge capital that can fuel economic growth.

The fact is, we have not been maintaining what we have, much less building for the future. Here's an example.

If I want to take the Amtrak from Portland, Oregon, to Seattle, Washington, the journey will be from one antiquated station to another. At an average speed of a bit better than forty miles per hour, the trip of 160 miles will take nearly four hours, if it is not delayed. And at those times when the engine does actually get up over fifty miles per hour, you don't want to be walking in the aisle unless you have a good sense of balance and a cat-like ability to catch yourself from getting flung on top of another passenger, such is the stability of an Amtrak train at freeway speed.

As a nation, we are under-investing, running down our assets and infrastructure, and squandering opportunities for economic growth now and in the future. Our aging infrastructure is simply wearing out.

By comparison, China is building strategic growth markets. From nuclear power to aircraft manufacturing, the Chinese are using the power of their budget and the size of their (future) market to define the rules of the game for multinationals the world over. In the process, China is skillfully extracting technological know-how, forcing investment in their economy (jobs), and returning very little for it. They will build industries, create jobs, and define entire ecosystems of products and services that we will miss out on because we lacked the political imagination to get past ideology or to leverage the power of government to build and invest in the infrastructure of a twenty-first-century nation.

Not everything is rosy for China, however. The July 2011 wreck of two high-speed rail trains demonstrated that a lot of the infrastructure China has rushed to build is of substandard quality. China is an extreme case. They are overbuilding and not doing it well. But America is the other extreme. We are running down what we have without building for the future.

Even as we grapple with our fiscal challenges, we are going to have to figure out how to significantly punch up spending on infrastructure, education, and the big and little science needed to make us wealthy in the future. We need the highways of tomorrow, high-speed rail in every high-density corridor that makes sense, and a step jump in internet broadband speed. We need to expand our research and development in both public and private sectors.

We are facing the reality of a new age of austerity and the need to make dramatic cutbacks in entitlements and, yes, to bear slightly higher taxes. We need to conduct that debate while understanding the strategic context of how and where we need to invest in order to be a twenty-first century country. We cannot be a great economic power with an infrastructure and educational system that are crumbling around us. We must make our decisions about taxes and spending with an awareness of how much we need to invest now to achieve prosperity tomorrow and the important role that government can and must play in making it happen.

CHAPTER 37

The Final Frontier: An Exploration Economy

When I was a kid, I recall reading *The High Frontier* by Gerard K. O'Neill, which promised that by now, we would be living in a future of orbiting space colonies and mining on the moon. Even a decade ago, Robert Zubrin was writing about *Entering Space*. The potential for humanity to become a space-faring civilization seemed within reach using today's technologies.

Austerity and reduced budgets have limited the means and pushed back the vision. By the time you read this, the Space Shuttle program will have ended and we'll be hitching rides with the Russians to get an astronaut in space. Yet America will certainly launch itself into space one day in grander fashion. It is only a matter of time.

I believe that we should be doing much more to develop the final frontier, a future in space where there are unlimited resources and opportunities for growth. I believe America should be investing in a more concerted effort to develop the underlying technologies to launch and sustain a large-scale presence throughout the solar system. I believe this effort will one day be deserving of a vastly larger budget than today's current NASA funding. And when I say *vastly larger*, I mean multiples of five or ten, although not from day one.

Mind you, I'm not a Trekkie and I don't have a light saber in my closet. I am not even all that interested in science fiction. What I am interested in is walled gardens.

If you don't know what a walled garden is, think Apple. Apple is an example of a company that has created a tightly bound, proprietary ecosystem of products ranging from iPods to iPhones to iPads all interacting with Apple's iTunes store and soon to be iCloud offerings. Apple has created a walled garden. You can't really use your products outside of Apple's walled garden, and competitors are at a loss because they cannot easily duplicate the attractiveness of what Apple has created or step inside to steal Apple's customers. Walled gardens translate into big profits. Apple is now one of the largest companies by market capitalization in the world.

In my mind, a robust space program is a walled garden whose productive capabilities are bound up with defense-related industries and cannot be easily breached by offshore competitors. (Translation: The jobs stay here.) We can and should protect them on national security grounds. I urge a new space-industrial complex that would be funded by redirecting and downsizing the military-industrial complex in direct proportion. The synergy between the two ought to allow for such a transition and would easily keep our technical mastery in the defense industry, should we face a real threat in the future.

For many, this will sound like an implausible science fiction vision, but the time for this is coming sooner than you think. There will be a moment in our generation that electrifies our imaginations and our politics. I'd like to think it occurs when we discover a true earth-like world orbiting some far away star.

But that won't be it. The turning point for the future of the American space program will occur when a Chinese astronaut lands on the moon and plants the flag of an authoritarian regime. Gone will be the use of Sputnik as a rhetorical device for how other countries *could* surpass us. This will be the real thing, and it will ignite a maelstrom of debate and self-flagellation within America over the question of who lost the moon more than a half century after we got there first. We are a nation in which 58 percent of Americans believe it is essential to be a world leader in space exploration and 750,000 people turned out to watch the last launch of Atlantis.[23] Every politician and party will be forced to explain how we lost the moon.

I personally can't wait. Nothing will rally America faster than a challenge that clearly and visibly shows we have lost the lead and squandered an opportunity that was ours and ours alone. After losing ground in everything from the fastest computer to the fastest trains, the highest-scoring students to the highest production of solar cells, I suspect this is the big one that will spark the outrage and consensus to deal with our failures.

We need to invest, massively, in launch systems, propulsion systems, lunar and asteroid mining, power generation, habitat construction, deep space science and engineering, and the big science of astrophysics. This will require engineering in complex and challenging new environments. As a result, new industries will form. We will have jobs focused on manufacturing in space, mining the asteroids and the moon, and producing energy on a large scale above orbit. Vast returns are possible from such efforts, as is unlimited economic growth. Preparing the infrastructure for a major move into the final frontier and all its possibilities is an important contributor to building a fast-growing economy and leading industries for the year 2050, and it's even more critical for the fifty years beyond that.

At a minimum, it is time to start laying down the blueprint for how we will get there. This will require a far larger, more sustainable vision than the few manned missions and outposts currently envisioned.

CHAPTER 38

A New War on Poverty

WE NEED A NEW war on poverty around the world. This action is one of the most tangible demonstrations that we care about the poor wherever they are. It builds brand America, increases our soft power, and will improve our global standing in a future when we will have to work harder to persuade and inspire other countries to follow us.

We have long contributed to this great cause, but too often our aid comes with strings attached—in the form of requirements to hire American consultants or purchase American goods, such as our farm surpluses—making it less useful for the job at hand and less appreciated by those in need. We need to reevaluate our approach to how much we give (more would be better, but less is likely, given the budget challenges we face), how we give (fewer consultants and strings attached), and to increase our aid so that we can set the bar higher for and draw contrasts with other countries that currently only act in their own self-interest.

There are many ways to pursue this, whether through aid from institutions like United States Agency for International Development (USAID) and the World Bank; trade, FDI, and outsourcing from the private sector; or through the vast array of foundations around the world engaged in lending a hand. But I think our most valuable and cost-effective asset is our people, and one institution I know well that remains one of the best suited for showing American values in action is the Peace Corps.

Peace Corps—Return to the Bold Experiment

When it emerged in the 1960s, the Peace Corps was called a 'bold experiment.' There was an aura of excitement about it. There was vitality and energy in everything it did and represented.

Today, when I see editorials about the Peace Corps, they are invariably on an anniversary and typically use words like *laudable* and *venerable*—words intended, I suppose, to convey respect and appreciation. For the record, I hate such words. I don't mean to be ungenerous, for their intent is not unkind. But if those are the words that come to mind when people think about the Peace Corps today, then it is ample evidence that the agency has become a pale shadow of what it once was and could be again. We need to put *bold* and *experiment* back into the Peace Corps.

No other agency within the federal government has as much potential to show the best side of Americans than this one. What we need is to scale it up. This is no easy matter. Every president since Reagan has been challenging the Peace Corps to grow to 10,000 volunteers overseas (it typically has about 8,000 volunteers serving around the world at any point in time). George W. Bush even suggested 14,000 in one State of the Union Address. Not once in thirty years has the agency met the challenge. To me, the failure to exceed 10,000 is a sign that the agency has failed to live up to its promise. Eventually, the politicians will stop looking to the Peace Corps to represent America's effort to make the world a better place.

In a world where poverty limits the potential of billions of people, numbers matter. From literacy to poverty, environment to AIDs, scale matters. Being a drop in the ocean does not change the sea, no matter how noble of a drop it is.

Scale is possible. Real-world proof comes from the unlikely source of Cuba's volunteers in Venezuela. There have reportedly been as many as 20,000 Cubans serving in grassroots development work in poor communities throughout Venezuela. Conservatives have taken a dim view of what these people are doing, and they may be right. The point is that if the Cubans can manage to field 20,000 people working in poor communities in one single country, why can't our beloved Peace Corps manage more than 8,000 for the entire world? What the Cubans have have done is destroy the idea that there is any natural limit on the number of volunteers that could be working in a country where there is a large number of poor that need help.

The US administration needs to put in place a leadership that is activist, bold, and capable of reinvigorating the Peace Corps and will challenge many of its bedrock assumptions about what it can and can't do. I suspect that the agency has settled into a comfort zone. And while funding is an issue, challenging orthodoxy is a fundamental precept to breaking through glass ceilings. Twenty thousand US Peace Corps volunteers working overseas would be a boon for America's image abroad. Forty thousand might actually make a meaningful difference if targeted on specific causes. If we start to think at scale, interesting things are possible.

South Africa has long faced the challenge of overcoming the legacy of apartheid. There are less than two hundred volunteers in South Africa today. I'm sure every one of them is doing a great job. But why aren't there 1,000, 2,000, or more? Do two hundred volunteers really meet the need of millions of people living in poverty?

We don't have any volunteers in Brazil. What if we offered 1,000 or 2,000 volunteers to work in the Amazon basin on conservation activities—the front line of the battle against global warming?

We don't have any volunteers in India today. What if we offered to put 2,000 volunteers at work in rural villages helping the rural poor improve their lives?

Some countries like India and Brazil may see themselves as rising powers in their own right and be reluctant to admit they have challenges that need an agency like the Peace Corps. What if we challenged these rising new countries to jointly field clusters of volunteers made up of Americans, Chinese, Indians, and Brazilians in these countries as well as jointly all across Africa, Latin America, and Asia?

There is no shortage of need or opportunities to do something. There is also no shortage of American volunteers willing to go, especially in these hard economic times. Peace Corps routinely used to get 250,000 calls, to which it sent 50,000 applications and received 10,000 to 20,000 completed applications. There are more than enough Americans interested to field 40,000 to 50,000 volunteers around the world. We have barely tried to call them to service. If we call, they will come in large numbers.

It's time to energize the Peace Corps. What is needed is the creativity, imagination, and will to use America's best resource—its people—to achieve truly significant gains in the war that matters most to people all over the world—the one on poverty.

CHAPTER 39

Summarizing the Big Ideas

WHAT I HAVE OFFERED in this section is a set of big initiatives that I think will contribute significantly to the goal of economic growth characterized by rapid growth in median income. This is the path, albeit incomplete, to the 5 percent nation.

Here's a quick summary with some rough estimate of what it will all cost:

The most important link between our current position and higher wages is education and skill. We need to create a New Educational Frontier that dramatically improves our people's skills. We need to do this with a University of America that puts a college education within the reach of every American at a fraction of the cost of today's four-year degree. We need to do it by quickly reinforcing our K–12 teachers with a national program of teaching assistants that will ensure all children get the attentions they need to graduate at the peak of their potential and that leverages one of our greatest assets—the educational attainment of our retiring baby boomers (who are increasingly in need of additional income in retirement).

The cost of the University of America is probably in the range of $1 to $2 billion per year, cheap in the scheme of things. The cost of a national teaching assistant program is much bigger—approximately $40 billion. It may be that the cost of this can be recovered or partially funded by tying Social Security or other entitlement payments to seniors' willingness to provide volunteer services in our schools, a spin on fee-for-service.

If we can revolutionize how we approach education in America, then we can develop the most skilled workforce in the world, drive increased productivity, and create the potential for economic growth and higher wages far into the future.

We need to write a New Social Contract by helping our citizens face up to a future of rapid economic and technological changes that mean companies will come and go at a faster rate than ever before. We can do so by providing wage insurance and universal health care. Making sure every American knows we have their back will mean no American has to be afraid that our country is competing globally. The cost of a wage insurance program that covers every American can be relatively modest depending on how it is structured and financed. A modest payroll deduction and a restructuring of current unemployment insurance means the price tag could either net out or total $1 to $3 billion per year.

Universal health care is trickier. I go with the total price to consumers and businesses and believe if we could get even close to a European model, it would result in a net return of resources, potentially significant, to the bottom line of companies of all sizes and families at all economic levels across America.

Growing America means opening the door to greater levels of immigration in America. We should shoot for a population upwards of 500 million by 2050 and an economy that is significantly larger as a result. Immigration can help us reduce the challenges of an aging population and inspire the growth that will help us ameliorate public debt and future fiscal crises. Immigrants provide the vitality that we need to drive economic growth in every sector of our economy from housing to retail. Immigrants start businesses. They create jobs for the rest of us. They also work in our businesses as valued employees. We need more of them. The cost for this won't be free, but it will be more than offset by the increased economic growth immigrants add to our economy.

Doubling Exports is another priority. There are many good policies and programs that can help. I've focused on what it will take to unleash America's animal spirits of competition. I believe that means getting businesspeople out into the markets of the future—from China to India, Brazil to Eastern Europe—and pairing them up with a greatly expanded Commercial Service that serves as the single point of contact for all export promotion programs. The cost for the program I've outlined ranges from $2 to $3 billion per year with the goal of generating hundreds of billions in future additional exports.

We need a Green Revolution to promote and expand the use of green technologies in America. While we have dithered over the debate about global warming, China has seized the day and become a global leader in key industries. They now make 50 percent of all solar panels and 50 percent of all wind turbines. This is a short-sighted mistake on our part. We need to do better. There are many policies and initiatives that need to be done in this space. I have focused on the need to bridge the gap over environmental views while making markets more efficient. I have also presented a plan to put the power to influence corporate supply chains directly in consumers' hands by utilizing carbon labels and increasing the public's awareness of them. There is little to no cost for this, as I see it primarily as a nonprofit-driven mission.

We need to shoot for a Zero Deficit to end the biggest long-term threat to our own prosperity as well as the global economy—our addiction to deficit financing. By putting in place a balanced mix of taxes and spending that eliminates deficits, we can inspire confidence in our business community to start investing and creating jobs, to regain our standing in the world, and to rebuild Americans' faith that democracy works and our system of government can be effective. We cannot implement this with a Big Bang approach, given our current economic fragility, but we should begin to chart a clear path that is achievable within the next five years. The Simpson–Bowles committee provided a blueprint and template for how to do this. In the summer of 2011, we missed out on a grand bargain to improve our financial picture and suffered the consequence of a downgrade to our credit rating as a result. We need to do better.

We need to foster Strategic Growth Markets by building twenty-first-century markets. This means making investments to patch our crumbling infrastructure—from highways to bridges—and putting in place the highways of the future, the high-speed rail that is possible today, and a step change in broadband access. We will need to begin a massive shift in our federal expenditures to do this. We need to build national markets and to grow industries rather than just promote consumption and debt. Balancing our budget will need to include funds for investments such as the above.

We also need to invest in the biggest Strategic Growth Market of the future—the Final Frontier. We need to begin investing far more significantly in science and engineering that will lead humanity to a large, sustained presence throughout our solar system. Such steps make sense for the long-term future of economic growth. It will become a crisis of confidence and a necessity when China lands a man on the moon and plants their own flag on its soil.

This will not be cheap, and I am estimating a future budget in the hundreds of billions. However, I believe much of this could be diverted from defense spending. Space-related investments increase our cutting-edge technology skills, which are directly applicable to defense-related products. It ought to be possible to pay for this program by ramping down the military-industrial complex as we ramp up a space-industrial one, essentially a lateral shift that can always shift back in times of threat.

Finally, America needs to lead a New War on Poverty overseas in a larger, more visible way that will demonstrate our values to the world. This will be more important in the years ahead as we face a strong competitor that will challenge us at every turn. We will no longer be able to force countries into doing what we want. We will need to persuade them of our virtues and leadership. I've argued that a far bolder and more dynamic Peace Corps would also be one of the best and most cost-effective assets we could have in this effort. The incremental cost for ramping up this agency in a significant way is less than $1 billion.

Chapter 40

The Outsourcing Challenge

THROUGHOUT THIS BOOK, I've found that outsourcing represents a small share, around 2 percent, of the broader activity of job loss, change, and churn throughout the US economy as companies rise and fall, industries are created and destroyed, and people are forced to restart careers and lives as a result. I've outlined a broad set of policy ideas that would make people more resilient in the face of such changes, regardless of their cause, from a powerful set of educational options to a better social safety net. I've also targeted a set of policies that I think would grow our economy faster, resulting in more opportunities for all. But I can't end this book without a few final thoughts about outsourcing's impact on our economy and lives and some tentative ideas about how individuals can manage their careers in the years ahead in an age of more of the same: globalization, outsourcing, and rapid technology change.

Earlier in this book, I referenced an article by Alan Blinder in *Foreign Affairs* that speaks of the potential for all our manufacturing jobs to go offshore (14 million at the time of the article) and as many as two to three times that number of service jobs over the next few decades (30 to 45 million). He defines the vulnerable jobs as any type of work that does not require personal, in-person services in industries ranging from retail to health care. His prediction, should it come to pass, would truly represent a new industrial revolution, and it bears careful consideration. However, I am less sure that outsourcing will have this level of impact on the American economy going forward.

Let's start with a few surprises and unexpected conclusions about the future of outsourcing that I learned while writing this book. They help put into context some of the challenges we face, and I offer them in the form of four predictions.

Prediction 1

The flight of manufacturing jobs offshore will halt or reverse.

Global supply chains have never been cheap or easy to run. It's true that there is and has been cheaper labor overseas, but this advantage has always been partially offset by the cost of everything from transportation to logistics in producing from afar. You have to have more inventory in the pipeline—on ship, rail, and truck—on the way to the consumer or factory than if it were produced locally or just in time (all of which costs real money). These costs have always been significant, but they have been rising over time. Now, a series of elite management consulting groups, from McKinsey Global Institute to the Boston Consulting Group (BCG), have started saying the same thing: the economics of extended supply chains have started to turn.

An increasing trend and focus on agile manufacturing also requires suppliers to be located next to the factories they serve rather than in distant locations. This is impacting how some businesses think about their supply chains and where they want their suppliers located at the same time as the economics of them are becoming less attractive.

Finally, Chinese industry is set to begin a large wave of overseas investments, which will see factories move onshore and result in some increased employment in the countries they migrate to.

What all of this means is that there is a big structural change afoot that will provide a boost to manufacturing jobs in America. That doesn't mean everything will come back. Labor-intensive products like textiles, toys, and consumer electronics may not return. But some types of manufacturing—parts suppliers, customized components—do look set to come home in some reasonably significant way.

Prediction 2

Outsourcing nations may suffer more job losses than Americans as companies consolidate in the future.

Companies merge and acquire other companies all the time. When they do, they look for synergies and cost savings—and this means layoffs. It seems those layoffs have always affected Americans. We've been bearing the brunt of these hits for a generation. But that may not be the case going forward. The AOL example of 900 jobs lost, but just 200 hundred here in the United States may well be a harbinger of things to come.

Large companies have been globalizing their workforces for years. I've seen some suggestions that large companies already have on average 30 percent of their IT workforces outsourced. There is probably an upper limit to how much farther they will and can go. In fact, in 2005, McKinsey Global Institute calculated a theoretical maximum for the percentage of jobs in some sectors that could be offshored. In IT services, they estimated it was 44 percent. In IT packaged software, it was 49 percent.[24] We are getting close to those top-end numbers in the largest companies. At the same time, many back-office functions have also gone offshore in significant numbers among large companies.

In the future, when two big companies merge and start looking for synergies, they will undoubtedly compare notes on which vendor is providing back-office support. They won't need two big Indian workforces processing their accounts payable going forward. They won't need two big IT workforces offshore when they consolidate their IT systems. The ax isn't just going to fall on America anymore.

My second prediction, therefore, is that we may see more global job losses like the AOL example in the future with an increasing brunt of change falling overseas.

Prediction 3

Outsourcing nations may suffer more job losses than Americans as technology advances.

Outsourcing destination countries like India have benefited from advancing technology for nearly a generation, but they will face more consequences in the future. What I mean by this is that advances in artificial intelligence and software automation will hit IT and BPO jobs that have been offshored disproportionately. Many simple, repetitive tasks will become redundant. After all, automating a function is almost always less expensive than hiring lower-cost labor, and the simplest things to automate are tasks that are simple and repetitive.

For instance, call centers look exceptionally vulnerable to artificial intelligence. Imagine a more refined version of the Watson computer that can answer most simple questions equally as well as an offshore call center worker reading from a script. Many of the simplest call center transactions and services have been offshored. I suspect many of those will get automated away within the next five to ten years.

There are still call center jobs in the United States, and they are vulnerable, but US-based call centers tend to focus on higher touch, more valuable interactions and higher value, more demanding customers. The people able to do this type of transaction are the ones that will likely be retained.

Call centers are just one example. Anything simple and repetitive can be automated. Much of it will be.

Prediction 4

The economics of offshoring services will slowly change over time.

Just as the economics of manufacturing supply chains look set to rebalance global supply chains, the changing economics of labor supply and cost in locations like India look set to have a similar impact on service jobs in the IT and BPO space.

We have seen years of double-digit wage increases in India. Meanwhile, wages in the United States have stagnated or even fallen in some low-cost areas. Wages in India and other developing countries are still lower than in the United States, but the gap is closing. Over time the attractiveness of using offshore workers will begin to lessen.

Significantly, Indian outsourcing companies are starting to say exactly this. Recently the head of Genpact, a large outsourcing firm based in India, said that the cost of hiring an American to work in a call center is almost the same as an Indian, at least in some parts of the United States. He predicted that Indian firms would aggressively increase their American workforces in the years ahead and that Genpact would triple its existing US workforce of 1,500.[25]

Small increases add up over time, and the math of moving offshore will likely begin to change over time. I suspect fewer jobs will go overseas in the coming years based purely on labor cost.

Planning for Change

What all these predictions seem to suggest is that the pace of outsourcing and its impact on jobs here in the United States could begin to moderate in the years ahead. We could be near or even over the hump. There is no guarantee that this will occur. There are other trends that I may not be aware of that may accelerate the drive to outsource more offshore. But the trends I am aware of seem to point toward a moderation in the years ahead.

So what does this mean for Americans? Our odds of losing a job from outsourcing may be lessening, but this does not necessarily mean the odds of losing a job from any of the many sources of change—from technology innovations to industry competition and consolidation—are getting any smaller. So how do we survive job churn and change, whether the cause is from outsourcing or any other reason?

Personal advice is always more challenging and risky than talking about trends in aggregate, but I'll offer a couple of suggestions.

Here are my four basic recommendations: be paranoid, create a Plan B, save, and learn. These are pretty generic, and you can likely find them in some more highly developed form or fashion in just about any self-help book on the market, but I will try nevertheless.

Paranoia in our current economy should be pretty well acculturated, but the assumption you will lose a job at some point is a fundamental basis for surviving the change. Assuming it can and will happen means being responsible *now* for thinking through what you need to do and developing a plan to cope with it. The other three recommendations go into more detail on what to do. I see this step as being mentally prepared— to get motivated to do something ahead of time and to avoid some of the harmful outcomes referenced early on in this book such as depression, anger, or blaming yourself if and when it does happen.

Create a Plan B. Think through what you will do when this job and career ends, and have a plan for what you will do next. Start on that path now, not when you lose your job. Mind you, I appear to have chosen writing as a second career, which is possibly the world's most unreliable way to make an income. Having an MBA, I'm capable of running the numbers. The ROI is horrendous. I'm not offering myself up as a role model. Hopefully your Plan B will make better financial sense.

Not long ago I got into a conversation with a colleague who confessed a desire to one day own and run an ice cream shop. She was working so hard that it seemed to be a distant and unobtainable dream. But in talking it over, there were some tangible things she could do to start preparing: Talk to ice cream shop owners. Identify a location and see where the competition is. Look for formats that work. Experiment with recipes. Begin working on a business plan and understand what it is going to take to get started and how much it is possible to earn. Think of creative ways to do it part time (i.e., a weekend food cart in the summer), and build a fan base.

You don't have to go all in on your Plan B from the start. In fact, most Plan Bs are best served by starting as hobby projects to see if you can build on them and make them successful. That said, there is a difference between pursuing a hobby and a Plan B. A hobby that has no chance of ever turning into a job may be a dangerous luxury if it blinds you to the need to have and develop a back-up plan that can become a job in the future.

Save. This is the insult to injury if you are already stretched to the bone and struggling to make the monthly mortgage or rent. But it is the unavoidable truth. Do all you can to save and have a cushion for the day the sky falls in. The pain is not quite as severe if you aren't going to lose the house next month.

Finally, leverage savings to build skills. This is the other side of the Plan B. We all need to go back to school and learn more, to get a higher degree. I wish our country already had a University of America that would make this step more affordable for all of us. But education is still the most important investment we can make in ourselves, and it keeps skills fresh and relevant in this ever changing economy.

At the end of a hard day, it's all too easy to sit down in front of the TV or computer and zone out. But it's critically important to budget a few of those evenings a week for learning something new, adding a skill, or developing your Plan B.

While I'm convinced that outsourcing is not our biggest problem, I definitely understand that this is no comfort to a workforce and middle class under increasing strain and facing the challenges outlined earlier, namely wage stagnation, income inequality, economic insecurity, and a loss of social mobility. My hope is that the context and predictions laid out here will provide some comfort about where this particular revolution in business practice—outsourcing—is going and perhaps will make it a little less threatening.

CHAPTER 41

China Thoughts

CHINA HAS LOOMED large in this story, and a few final thoughts are warranted. I don't believe we need to panic over China's rise and growing role in the world. And it's time to stop blaming China for troubles of our own making and choices that we are freely making about our politics, economy, and future.

That doesn't mean China won't give us some challenges. They are now. There will be more to come. It seems overly optimistic to believe that their rise will be as peaceful as we hope and they say.

But let's also be realistic. China's rise is not as inevitable or certain as it is made out to be. The steady rise of China's economy over the next forty years at an average growth rate of 5.6 percent seems a shoo-in now when compared to years of blistering double digit rates of economic expansion. It could happen. I'm personally skeptical it will.

China has vast challenges on every front, from political transition to economic change and social transformation. Their entire economy is grossly distorted toward investment and exports, an addiction that is reminiscent of our own recent bubble in real estate that led to the subprime fiasco—except their problem is actually much, much worse in scope and scale. A *New York Times* article in July 2011, suggested that as much as 70 percent of Chinese GDP is in real estate and infrastructure spending, virtually all of which is fueled by debt, a good share of which could end up defaulting.[26] Wuhan, for instance, has an eight-year supply of vacant housing and is building hundreds of thousands more apartments.

I'm in good company when suggesting we treat forecasts of future Chinese growth with caution. Martin Wolf of the *Financial Times* has suggested that the great transition ahead for China from an export- and investment-oriented economy to a more balanced, consumer-based economy will be a bumpy ride.[27] Nouriel Roubini, an economist who predicted the Great Recession, has been equally blunt in predicting a "meaningful probability" of a Chinese economic slowdown.[28] *The Economist* says much the same, noting that China's years ahead are fraught with big challenges both economically and politically.[29]

Yet slower growth will challenge the roots of social cohesion and political legitimacy in a country with a long history of brutal civil conflict and a fragile system of authoritarian rule. While democracies bend, dictatorships snap. Recent events in the Middle East should remind us of this. The Chinese government is certainly thinking about it too. In early 2011, an anonymous email calling for a political protest caused a massive crackdown on political rights and expression all across China, followed by a massive burst in spending on internal security. This isn't a sign of strength at the top. It's a sign of fear.

Mind you, I want China to succeed and prosper. And you should too. It would mean a better, more prosperous world for everyone, including America, if they do. It would mean more trade, more jobs, and more opportunities for all. That future and that world are highly desirable outcomes. I believe we should do all we can to help China succeed. It will require enormous patience on our part, but it is worth the effort.

China's rapid economic growth is going to be harder to sustain in the future. We should spend less time panicking about their rise and more time focused on fixing our problems and implementing the structural changes at home that will result in our own rapid economic growth.

CONCLUSION

I BEGAN THIS BOOK with a moral dilemma: is the outsourcing of jobs offshore good or bad for Americans? Is it really an either-or question—either we outsource jobs *or* be more successful in manufacturing or green jobs or something else?

I've outlined the costs and the benefits as fairly and objectively as I could, and I've been transparent about possible biases. I've taken a stand and given you my opinion, which is that outsourcing is a bit player in a larger drama of economic change. It appears to cost us just 2 percent of jobs each year, a modest number even if I've underestimated significantly. The benefits, from cheaper goods to better service, trade-related jobs to innovation companies, appear to outweigh the costs and could actually do so significantly. This looks true today, and I suspect it will be even more so in the future as emerging economies prosper and begin to draw in more imports.

If you've come with me this far, you are also now armed with the data and a set of frameworks yourself. You can decide differently. In fact, the data is always changing as we learn more. The case today (even assuming we agree on my interpretation of the data) may look dramatically different tomorrow, next year, or five years from now. It may get worse. It may get better.

But all that may not really matter—and this is the really interesting piece that makes this such a fascinating topic. I've also learned that most of us aren't going to change our opinion and—no offense intended—probably won't decide in a rational way anyway. We will go with our gut. And we aren't alone in this. Moral Foundations Theory offers some insights on why people will always have a gut reaction against the idea of jobs going to some other country (much less so if they go to North Dakota—at least there, they are American and part of the same national tribe). It's a violation of too many moral building blocks such as fairness, harm, and community/ingroup loyalty.

But it is also true that context matters to gut reactions. If people feel like the economy is growing and new jobs are plentiful, then the gut reacts less intensely. That is not the case today. That is why our gut reaction to outsourcing is as intensely negative as it is. (That is also, by the way, what makes us easy prey for politicians and pundits of all stripes on this topic. They know a hot button when they see one and have no compunction about pushing it for votes or ratings.)

But there is something much bigger going on. We face a daunting set of forces that have been bearing down on our middle class for a generation. We face a looming fiscal crisis, a creeping demographic trap, and a relative decline in our nation's influence and power. These outcomes are the result of forces that appear to be slowly undermining our economic strength, and many relate to globalization, rapid technology change, and, yes, outsourcing to a small but visible extent. Americans clearly sense these forces are at work, and this is driving their anxiety about outsourcing, our economy, their own personal future, and their faith in the American Dream.

In response, I've outlined a fairly aggressive agenda from education to a more effective social safety net that I think would increase the potential of our economy to grow at a faster rate than ever before and would keep us the largest economy and a global power through the remainder of this century. This growth and dynamism would create opportunities for Americans at every level. And that would change how Americans view our opportunities in the world and their potential to thrive and prosper in it. In effect, it would renew the license to operate for an open economy and would reduce calls for protectionism. It would also address some of the baseline fears that Americans have about the durability of the American Dream.

I don't believe our future is an either-or question—whether or not we want to be a country that outsources jobs or a country that is more prosperous. I believe America can succeed and prosper in a fast-changing world characterized by globalization, outsourcing, and rapid technology change. I believe America has an extraordinary future ahead of it. Our decline in relative power is a product of our success in shaping the world the way we wanted it to be. We should see this for what it is:

a huge opportunity. The story of our age is hundreds of millions of our fellow humans emerging from poverty, and we should do everything we can to expand that storyline.

I believe we can and will manage the new global order and build a shared prosperity for all. We can and will manage the process of saving the planet and its environment. Other powers may rise, but we remain the leader of the free world and this is our challenge and our responsibility. I believe we are up for it.

NOTES

Introduction

1 Daniel Yankelovich, "The Tipping Points," *Foreign Affairs* 85:3 (May/June 2006): 119.

2 German Marshall Fund, "Perspectives on Trade and Poverty Reduction: A Survey of Public Opinion, Key Findings Report 2007" (2007): 21–22, www.gmfus.org.

3 The Pew Research Center for the People & the Press, "Even as Optimism About Iraq Surges, Declining Public Support for Global Engagement" (September 24, 2008): 1.

4 The Pew Research Center for the People and the Press, "Americans Are of Two Minds on Trade: More Trade, Mostly Good; Free Trade Pacts, Not So" (November 9, 2010), www.pewresearch.org/pubs/1795/poll-free-trade-agreements-jobs-wages-economic-growth-china-japan-canada.

5 Lou Dobbs, *War on the Middle Class: How the Government, Big Business, and Special Interest Groups Are Waging War on the American Dream and How to Fight Back* (New York: Penguin Group, 2006), 10.

6 Business Week, "The Future of Outsourcing" (January 30, 2006):1, http://www.businessweek.com/magazine/content/06_05/b3969401.html

7 Adam Nishinsky, Fortune Magazine, Keynote address, Outsourcing World Summit 2006, International Association of Outsourcing Professionals, Orlando, FL, February, 2006).

8 Thomas Friedman, *Hot, Flat, and Crowded: Why We Need a Green Revolution and How it Can Renew America,* (New York: Farrar, Straus and Giroux, 2008), 23.

9 Michael F. Corbett, *The Outsourcing Revolution: Why It Makes Sense and How to Do It Right* (Chicago: Dearborn Trade Publishing, 2004), 7.

10 Pew Research Center for the People and the Press, "Strengthen Ties with China, But Get Tough on Trade" (January 12, 2011), www.pewresearch.org/pubs/1855/china-poll-americans-want-closer-ties-but-tougher-trade-policy.

PART 1

Overview

1 Ben Heineman, ed., China: The Balance Sheet, What the World Needs to Know About the Emerging Superpower (New York: Public Affairs, 2006), 105.

2 Dragnomics,"Foreign Exports: Computer Age," China Economic Quarterly Q2 (2006), 27.

Chapter 1

3 Robert J. Lalonde, "The Case for Wage Insurance," Council on Foreign Relations, CSR No. 30 (September 2007), 8.

4 Debbie Borie-Holtz, Carl Van Horn, Cliff Zukin, "No End in Sight: The Agony of Prolonged Unemployment," Rutgers University (May 2010), 6, www.heldrich.rutgers.edu/uploadedFiles/Publications/Work_Trends_21_May_2010.pdf.

5 Peter Gosselin, *High Wire: The Precarious Financial Lives of American Families* (New York: Basic Books, 2008), 85–87.

6 Louis Uchitelle, *The Disposable American: Layoffs and Their Consequences* (New York: Alfred A. Knopf, 2006), 179–180.

7 Debbie Borie-Holtz, Carl Van Horn, Cliff Zukin, "No End in Sight: The Agony of Prolonged Unemployment," Rutgers University (May 2010), 6, www.heldrich.rutgers.edu/uploadedFiles/Publications/Work_Trends_21_May_2010.pdf.

8 Bureau of Labor Statistics, "Private Sector Gross Job Gains and Losses, Seasonally Adjusted" (2009), Table 1, www.bls.gov/news.release/cewbd.t01.htm

9 Bureau of Labor Statistics, "Annual Layoffs and Discharges Levels (1) by Industry and Region, Not Seasonally Adjusted" (January 2009), Table 17, www.bls.gov/news.release/jolts.t17.htm.

10 Bureau of Labor Statistics, "Mass Layoff Statistics," www.bls.gov/MLS/.

11 Bureau of Labor Statistics, "Extended Mass Layoffs in the Fourth Quarter of 2007 and Annual Totals for 2007" (February 14, 2008), www.bls.gov/news.release/archives/mslo_02142008.pdf.

12 Bureau of Labor Statistics, "Job Openings and Labor Turnover: January 2009" (March 10, 2009), 24, www.bls.gov/news.release/archives/jolts_03102009.pdf.

13 Bureau of Labor Statistics, "Extended Mass Layoffs Archives, 2009," www.bls.gov/schedule/archives/mslo_nr.htm#2010

14 Working America and the AFL-CIO, "Outsourced: Sending Jobs Overseas: The Cost to America's Economy and Working Families" (2010), 10, www.workingamerica.org/upload/OutsourcingReport.pdf.

15 Ajay Goel, Nazgol Moussavi, and Vats N.Srivatsan, "Time to Rethink Offshoring?," McKinsey Quarterly (September 2008), www.mckinseyquarterly.com/Time_to_rethink_offshoring_2190.

16 RSM McGladrey, "2008 Manufacturing and Wholesale Distribution National Survey" (2008), www.rsmmcgladrey.com/index.php?/Manufacturing-Wholesale-Distribution/RSM-McGladrey-Annual-Manufacturing-and-Wholesale-Distribution-Survey.

17 The Boston Consulting Group, "Made in the USA, Again: Manufacturing Is Expected to Return to America as China's Rising Labor Costs Erase Most of the Savings from Offshoring" (May 5, 2011), www.bcg.com/media/PressReleaseDetails.aspx?id=tcm:12-75973.

18 Michael E. Porter and Jan W. Rivkin, "Choosing the United States," Special Report: Reinventing America, *Harvard Business Review* (March, 2012), p. 80-93.

19 Diana Farrell and Jaeson Rosenfeld, "US Offshoring: Rethinking the Response," McKinsey Global Institute (December 2005), 2, www.mckinsey.com/mgi/reports/pdfs/rethinking/US_Offshoring_Rethinking_the_Response.pdf.

20 Nasscom, "Nasscom Strategic Review 2009," www.nasscom.org/upload/60452/Executive_summary.pdf; Nasscom, "Nasscom Strategic Review 2008," www.nasscom.org/Nasscom/templates/NormalPage.aspx?id=53454.

21 Nasscom, "Nasscom Strategic Review 2010," 6, www.nasscom.in/upload/SR10/ExecutiveSummary.pdf.

22 Alan S. Blinder, "Offshoring: The Next Industrial Revolution?" Foreign Affairs 85 (March/April 2006), 113.

23 James Lamont, "US Proves Call Centre Match for India Over Hire Costs," Financial Times (August 18, 2010).

Chapter 2

24 Robert B. Reich, "The Anxious Middle Class in Work and Retirement" (statement of Secretary of Labor Robert B. Reich before the Subcommittee on Deficits, Debt Management and Long-Term Growth, Senate Committee on Finance, December 7, 1994), www.dol.gov/oasam/programs/history/reich/congress/120794rr.htm.

25 Stephen Greenhouse, "Tough Times for American Workers," San Francisco Chronicle (April 11, 2008).

26 Jared Bernstein, "Median Income Rose as Did Poverty in 2007; 2000s Have Been Extremely Weak for Living Standards of Most Households," Economic Policy Institute (August 26, 2008), www.epi.org/publications/entry/webfeatures_econindicators_income_20080826/.

27 Pew Research Center for the People and the Press, "Americans Are of Two Minds on Trade: More Trade, Mostly Good; Free Trade Pacts, Not So" (November 9, 2010), www.pewresearch.org/pubs/1795/poll-free-trade-agreements-jobs-wages-economic-growth-china-japan-canada.

28 Economic Policy Institute, "State of Working America 2008/2009" (2008), 7, www.stateofworkingamerica.org/swa08_00_execsum.pdf.

29 Robert Z. Lawrence, "Blue-Collar Blues: Is Trade to Blame for Rising US Income Inequality?" Peterson Institute for International Economics (2008), 27–46.

30 McKinsey Global Institute, "Changing the Fortunes of America's Workforce: A Human Capital Challenge" (June 2009), 10, www.mckinsey.com/mgi/publications/changing_fortunes/index.asp.

31 Motoko Rich, "Factory Jobs Return, but Employers Find Skills Shortage," *The New York Times* (July 1, 2010), www.nytimes.com/2010/07/02/business/economy/02manufacturing.html.

32 The Henry J. Kaiser Family Foundation, "Health Care Costs: A Primer" (March 2009), www.kff.org/insurance/index.cfm.

33 National Center for Public Policy and Higher Education, "Measuring Up 2008: The National Report Card on Higher Education" (2008), 8, www.measuringup2008.highereducation.org/.

34 Pew Research Center for the People and the Press, "Inside the Middle Class: Bad Times Hit the Good Life" (April 9, 2008), 6–11, www.pewsocialtrends.org/assets/pdf/MC-Middle-class-report.pdf.

35 Alan S. Blinder, "Offshoring: The Next Industrial Revolution?" *Foreign Affairs* 85:2 (March/April 2006), 123.

Chapter 3

36 Peter Navarro, *The Coming China Wars: Where They Will Be Fought. How They Can Be Won* (Upper Saddle River, NJ: Pearson Education, Inc., 2007), 11.

37 China Labor Watch, www.chinalaborwatch.org/.

38 China Labour Bulletin, www.clb.org.hk/en/.

39 Alexandra Harney, *The China Price: The True Cost of Chinese Competitive Disadvantage* (New York: The Penguin Press, 2008), 219.

40 China Labour Bulletin, "China's Labour Dispute Resolution System," www.clb.org.hk/en/node/100618.

41 Edward Wong, "Global Crisis Adds to Surge of Labor Disputes in Chinese Courts," *The New York Times* (September 15, 2010), www.nytimes.com/2010/09/16/world/asia/16china.html?ref=global.

Chapter 4

42 Elizabeth Rosenthal, "China Increases Lead as Biggest Carbon Dioxide Emitter," *The New York Times* (June 14, 2008), www.nytimes.com/2008/06/14/world/asia/14china.html.

43 International Energy Agency, "World Energy Outlook 2008—Fact Sheet: Global Energy Trends" (2008), www.iea.org/weo/docs/weo2008/fact_sheets_08.pdf.

44 BBC News, "China Seeks Export Carbon Relief" (March 17, 2009), www.news.bbc.co.uk/2/hi/science/nature/7947438.stm

45 Richard McGregor, "Beijing Clouds the Pollution Picture," *Financial Times* (July 3, 2007), 2.

Chapter 5

46 Nikki Tait, "China the Main Culprit as EU Product Recalls Rise 53 Percent," *Financial Times* (April 18, 2008).

47 Associated Press, "Mattel Apologizes to China for Recalls," *The New York Times* (September 21, 2007).

48 Hari Bapuji and Andre Laplume, "Toy Recalls and China: One Year Later," *Asia Pacific Foundation Research Reports* (November 6, 2008), www.asiapacific.ca/sites/default/files/filefield/ToyRecallsUpdate_0.pdf.

Chapter 6

49 Staff Research Study 28, "The Effects of Increasing Chinese Demand on Global Commodity Markets," Office of Industries, U.S. International Trade Commission 3864 (June 2006), 1–3, www.hotdocs.usitc.gov/docs/pubs/research_working_papers/pub3864-200606.pdf.

50 Staff Research Study 28, "The Effects of Increasing Chinese Demand on Global Commodity Markets," Office of Industries, U.S. International Trade Commission 3864 (June 2006), 2–13, www.hotdocs.usitc.gov/docs/pubs/research_working_papers/pub3864-200606.pdf.

51 www.en.wikipedia.org/wiki/Price_of_petroleum

52 World Bank, "Global Economic Prospects 2009" (2009), 58.

53 Susan Lyon, Rebecca Lefton, and Daniel J. Weiss, "Quenching Our Thirst for Oil: Growing Global Oil Demand Harms U.S. Security and Economy," Center for American Progress (April 23, 2010), www.americanprogress.org/issues/2010/04/oil_quench.html.

54 Javier Blas and Leslie Hook, "China Set to Overtake Japan as Largest Importer of Thermal Coal," *Financial Times* (June 24, 2010).

55 Shai Oster, "China Ignites Global Coal Market," *The Wall Street Journal* (May 4, 2010), www.online.wsj.com/article/SB10001424052748703612804575222212477812190.html.

56 Shane Streifel, "Impact of China and India on Global Commodity Markets: Focus on Metals & Minerals and Petroleum," World Bank (n.d.), 19. http://siteresources.worldbank.org/INTCHIINDG LOECO/Resources/ChinaIndiaCommodityImpact.pdf

57 World Bank, "Global Economic Prospects 2009" (2009), 5–6.

58 FAO, IFAD, and WFP, "High Food Prices: Impact and recommendations" (paper prepared for the meeting of the Chief Executives Board for Coordination, International Fund for Agricultural Development (IFAD), Berne, Switzerland, April 28–29, 2008), www.ifad.org/operations/food/ceb.htm.

59 World Bank, "Global Economic Prospects 2009" (2009), 58.

60 World Bank, "Global Economic Prospects 2009" (2009), 4.

Chapter 7

61 *The Economist*, "A Special Report on China and its Region: The Export Juggernaut" (March 31, 2007), 11–12.

62 Tom Mitchell, "China's 'Workshop of the World' Suffers Acute Labour Shortage," Financial Times (February 26, 2010).

63 Jeffrey Becker and Manfred Eflstrom, "The Impact of China's Labor Contract Law on Workers," International Labor Rights Forum (May 12, 2010), 8, www.laborrights.org/sites/default/files/ publications-and-resources/ChinaLaborContractLaw2010_0.pdf .

64 Keith Bradsher, "China Takes Lead in Clean Energy, With Aggressive State Aid," The New York Times (September 8, 2010), www.nytimes.com/2010/09/09/business/global/09trade.html.

65 Peter Marsh, "India Set for Big Gain in Electronics Outsourcing," Financial Times (May 22, 2007), www.ft.com/cms/s/2/8b03dee2-0883-11dc-b11e-000b5df10621.html.

66 Alexandra Harney, *The China Price: The True Cost of Chinese Competitive Advantage* (New York: The Penguin Press, 2007), 19.

67 Haiyan Deng, Jianyi Xu, John Haltiwanger, Robert H. McGuckin III, Yaodong Liu, Yuqi Liu, "China's Productivity Boom: The Contribution of Restructuring to Growth and Competitiveness," The Conference Board, Research Report R-1411-07-RR (December 2007), 9, www.conference-board.org/publications/publicationdetail.cfm?publicationid=1386.

68 *The Economist,* "Lost in Translation" (May 19, 2007), 74.

69 William R. Cline and John Williamson, "Estimates of Fundamental Equilibrium Exchange Rates, May 2010," Peterson Institute for international Economics PB10-15 (June 2010), 7, www.piie.com/publications/pb/pb10-15.pdf.

70 Tom Orlik, "What's the Yuan Worth?" *The Wall Street Journal* (June 2, 2011), C8.

Chapter 8

71 Diana Farrell, Susan Lund, and Koby Sadan, "The New Power Brokers: Gaining Clout in Turbulent Markets," McKinsey Global Institute (July 2008).

72 Paul Krugman, "China's Dollar Trap," *The New York Times* (April 3, 2009).

73 Jamil Anderlini, "China Loses Billions on Equities Bets Ahead of Markets' Collapse," *Financial Times* (March 16, 2009).

74 Geoff Dyer, "China's Dollar Dilemma," *Financial Times* (February 22, 2009).

75 Sandeep Tucker, "China Aims to Buy Up Overseas Companies," *Financial Times* (May 31, 2007).

PART 2

Chapter 11

1 Fred C. Bergsten, "The United States in the World Economy," Petersen Institute (2005), cited in Scott C. Bradford, Paul L. E. Grieco, and Gary Clyde Hufbauer, "The Payoff to America from Global Integration," in *The United States and the World Economy*, ed. C. Fred Bersten (Washington, DC: Peterson Institute for International Economics, 2005), 68.

2 Business Planning Solutions, Global Insight Advisory Services Division , "The Price Impact of Wal-Mart: An Update Through 2006," Global Insight (September 4, 2007), 1–2.

Chapter 13

3 Organization for International Investment, "Insourcing Facts" (2010), www.ofii.org/resources/insourcing-facts.html.

4 Daniel H. Rosen and Thilo Hanneman, "An American Open Door: Maximizing the Benefits of Chinese Foreign Direct Investment," Asia Society and Woodrow Wilson International Center for Scholars (May 2011), 9, www.asiasociety.org/policy/center-us-china-relations/american-open-door.

5 Organization for International Investment, "The Impact on the U.S. Economy of Greenfield Projects by U.S. Subsidiaries of Foreign Companies—Top Projects for 2008" (March, 2009), 3, www.ofii.org/docs/Greenfield_2009_Report.pdf.

Chapter 14

6 James Fallows, "China Makes, the World Takes," *The Atlantic* (July/August 2007), 69, www.theatlantic.com/magazine/archive/2007/07/china-makes-the-world-takes/5987/.

7 Arik Hesseldahl, "The iPod is Dead. Long Live the iPod," *Business Week* (July 28, 2009), www.finance.yahoo.com/family-home/article/107415/the-ipod-is-dead-long-live-the-ipod.html.

8 Miguel Helft and Ashlee Vance, "Apple Passes Microsoft as No. 1 in Tech," *The New York Times* (May 26, 2010), www.nytimes.com/2010/05/27/technology/27apple.html?_r=1&hp.

9 Greg Linden, Jason Dedrick, Kenneth Kraemer, "Innovation and Job Creation in the Global Economy: The Case of Apple's iPod" (January 2009), 7–8, www.pcic.merage.uci.edu/papers/2008/InnovationAndJobCreation.pdf.

10 Christopher Lawton, Ykari Iwatanikane, and Jason Dean, "U.S. Upstart Takes on TV Giants in Price War," *Wall Street Journal* (April 15, 2008), www.online.wsj.com/public/article/SB120820684382013977.html.

11 Cliff Edwards, "How Vizio Beat Sony in High-Def TV," *BusinessWeek* (April 26, 2010), www.business week.com/magazine/content/10_18/b4176051946906.htm.

12 "Nike, Inc., Annual Report on Form 10-K" (2009), www.media.corporate-ir.net/media_files/irol/10/100529/AnnualReport/nike-sh09-rev2/docs/Nike_2009_10-K.pdf.

Chapter 15

13 Investment Company Institute and the Securities Industry Association, "Equity and Bond Ownership in America 2008" (2008), 1, www.ici.org/pdf/rpt_08_equity_owners.pdf.

14 Investment Company Institute and the Securities Industry Association, "Equity Ownership in America, 2005" (2005), 1, 12–13, www.ici.org/pdf/rpt_05_equity_owners.pdf.

15 OECD, "Pensions at a Glance 2009: Retirement-Income Systems in OECD Countries" (2009), www.oecd.org/els/social/pensions/PAG.

16 Employee Benefit Research Institute, "Retirement Confidence Survey 2009" (April 2009), www.ebri.org/pdf/briefspdf/EBRI_IB_4-2009_RCS1.pdf.

Chapter 16

17 Louis Uchitelle, *The Disposable American: Layoffs and Their Consequences* (New York: Alfred A. Knopf Publishing, 2006), 5.

Chapter 17

18 William Neumann, "Fostering China's Taste for Nuts," *The New York Times* (June 28, 2010), www.nytimes.com/2010/06/29/business/media/29nuts.html.

19 U.S. Census Bureau, "Trade in Goods with China" (2011), www.census.gov/foreign-trade/balance/c5700.html#2000.

20 McKinsey Global Institute, "From 'Made in China' to 'Sold in China': The Rise of the Chinese Urban Consumer" (November 2006), 1.

21 World Bank, "Global Economic Prospects, Managing the Next Wave of Globalization" (2007), xvi.

22 McKinsey Global Institute, "The 'Bird of Gold': The Rise of India's Consumer Market" (May 2007), 13–14.

23 AmCham-China, "AmCham-China Featured in USA Day News" (July 5, 2010), www.amchamchina.org/article/6579.

24 Bureau of Labor Statistics, "Occupational Outlook Handbook, 2010–11 Edition: Overview of the 2008–18 Projections (December 3, 2010), www.bls.gov/oco/oco2003.htm.

25 Bureau of Labor Statistics, "Industries at a Glance: Natural Resources and Mining," www.bls.gov/iag/natresmining.htm.

26 The National Mining Association, "Fast Facts About Coal," www.nma.org/statistics/fast_facts.asp.

27 Elizabeth Rosenthal, "Nations that Debate Coal Use Export It to Feed China's Need," *The New York Times* (November 22, 2010), www.nytimes.com/2010/11/22/science/earth/22fossil.html.

28 George Raine, "An Early Start for Longshore Contract Talks," San Francisco Chronicle (June 27, 2007), C1.

29 Robert Wright, "US Warned of Need to Expand Ports," *Financial Times* (June 11, 2007).

30 Andrew Ward, "Rail Tries to Keep Supplies in Track," *Financial Times* (July 27, 2006).

31 Laura M. Baughman and Joseph F. Francois, "Trade and American Jobs: The Impact of Trade on U.S. and State-Level Employment: An Update, For the Business Roundtable" (July 2010), www.businessroundtable.org/sites/default/files/JobsUpdate-FINAL.pdf.

Chapter 18

32 Wolf Martin, "The Recession Tracks the Great Depression" *Financial Times* (June 16, 2009).

33 David Leonhardt, "Part-Time Workers Mask Unemployment Woes," The New York Times (July 14, 2009), www.nytimes.com/2009/07/15/business/economy/15leonhardt.html?hp; Bureau of Labor Statistics, "Employment Situation Summary Table A: Household Data, Seasonally Adjusted," www.bls.gov/news.release/empsit.a.htm.

34 David Gelles, "AOL Cuts Workforce by 20 Percent," *Financial Times* (March 11, 2011).

35 Steve Lohr and John Markoff, "Computers Learn to Listen, and Some Talk Back," *The New York Times* (June 24, 2010), www.nytimes.com/2010/06/25/science/25voice.html.

36 Melissa Trujillo, "I, Robot—and Gardener: MIT Droid Tends Plants," Associated Press (April 10, 2009).

37 John Markoff, "Scientists Worry Machines May Outsmart Man," *The New York Times* (July 25, 2009), www.nytimes.com/2009/07/26/science/26robot.html.

Chapter 19

38 Lixin Fan, *Last Train Home,* Zeitgeist Films (2009), www.zeitgeistfilms.com/films/lasttrainhome/lasttrainhome.presskit.pdf.

39 Kathrin Hille, "Love You and Leave You," *Financial Times* (February 5–6, 2011), Life & Arts 1.

40 Leslie T. Chang, *Factory Girls: From Village to City in a Changing China* (New York: Spiegel & Grau, 2008), 11–13.

41 Leslie T. Chang, *Factory Girls: From Village to City in a Changing China* (New York: Spiegel & Grau, 2008), 370–372.

42 Jim Yardley, "Unelected Councils in India Run Villages With Stern Hand," The New York Times (June 5, 2011).

Chapter 20

43 German Marshall Fund, "Perspectives on Trade and Poverty Reduction: Key Findings Report 2006" (2006), 11, www.gmfus.org/doc/GMF_TradeSurvey percent202006.pdf.

44 United Nations, "Millenium Development Goals Report 2009" (2009), 4, www.un.org/millenniumgoals/pdf/MDG percent20Report percent202009 percent20ENG.pdf.

45 United Nations, "The Millenium Development Goals Report 2009" (2009), 7, www.un.org/millenni-umgoals/ pdf/MDG percent20Report percent202009 percent20ENG.pdf.-

46 United Nations, "The Millenium Development Goals Report 2010" (2010), 6–7, www.un.org/millenni-umgoals/pdf/MDG percent20Report percent202010 percent20En percent20r15 percent20-lowpercent20res percent2020100615 percent20-.pdf.

47 Nasscom, "Nasscom Strategic Review 2010" (2010), 6, www.nasscom.in/upload/SR10/ExecutiveSummary.pdf

48 Joe Leahy, "India's Private Sector Poised to Shore Up Infrastructure," *Financial Times* (April 27, 2007).

49 Peter Marsh, "India Set for Big Gain in Electronics Outsourcing," *Financial Times* (May 23, 2007).

PART 3
Chapter 21

1   Santa Clara University, "Markkula Center for Applied Ethics" (2010), www.scu.edu/ethics/.

2   Santa Clara University, "Markkula Center for Applied Ethics: Ethical Decision Making" (2010), www.scu.edu/ethics/practicing/decision/.

3   The Markkula Center for Applied Ethics, "Making an Ethical Decision" (2009), www.scu.edu/ethics/practicing/decision/making.pdf.

Chapter 26

4   Jonathan Haidt and Jesse Graham, "When Morality Opposes Justice: Conservatives Have Moral Intuitions that Liberals May Not Recognize," Social Justice Research, 2007.

5   Michael S. Gazzaniga, Human: The Science Behind What Makes Us Unique (New York: HarperCollins Publishers, 2008), 125.

6   Spassena Koleva, et al, "The Ties that Bind: How Five Moral Concerns Organize and Explain Political Attitudes" (draft manuscript under review, May 22, 2009), 12.

PART 4
Overview

1   Edward Luce, "Goodbye, American Dream," Financial Times (July 31, 2010).

2   Jacob S. Hacker, et al, "Economic Security at Risk: Findings from the Economic Security Index," The Rockefeller Foundation (July 2010), page ii.

3   Robert Reich, "How to End the Great Recession," The New York Times (September 2, 2010), www.nytimes.com/2010/09/03/opinion/03reich.html

4   U.S. Environmental Protection Agency, "Ag 101: Demographics" (2009), www.epa.gov/agriculture/ag101/demographics.html.

5   The Manufacturing Institute, "The Facts about Modern Manufacturing, 8th Edition" (2009), 14,
    www.nam.org/Statistics-And-Data/Facts-About-Manufacturing/~/media/0F91A0FBEA1847D087E71
    9EAAB4D4AD8.ashx.

6   The New York Times, "Smarter Than You Think" series (2010–2011),
    http://projects.nytimes.com/smarter-than-you-think.

Chapter 29

7   Rana Foroohar, "The 2 Percent Cconomy," Time Magazine (June 4, 2011),
    www.time.com/time/magazine/article/0,9171,2075364,00.html.

8   Uri Dadush and Bennett Stancil, "The World Order in 2050, Policy Outlook," The Carnegie Endowment
    for International Peace (April 2010), 8, www.carnegieendowment.org/files/World_Order_in_2050.pdf.

Chapter 30

9   John Michael Lee Jr. and Anita Rawls, "The College Completion Agenda: 2010 Progress Report,"
    College Board (July 2010), 10,
    www.completionagenda.collegeboard.org/sites/default/files/reports_pdf/Progress_Report_2010.pdf.

10 John Michael Lee Jr. and Anita Rawls, "The College Completion Agenda: 2010 Progress Report,"
    College Board (July 2010), 8,
    www.completionagenda.collegeboard.org/sites/default/files/reports_pdf/Progress_Report_2010.pdf.

11 College Board, "College Board Test" (2011), www.collegeboard.com/testing/.

12 Thomas G. Carroll, PhD and Elizabeth Foster, "Learning Teams: Creating What's Next," National
    Commission on Teaching and America's Future (April 2009),
    www.nctaf.org/documents/NCTAFLearningTeams408REG2-09_000.pdf.

13 Christopher B. Swanson, PhD, "Closing the Graduation Gap: Educational and Economic Conditions in
    America's Largest Cities," Editorial Projects in Education (April 2009),
    www.americaspromise.org/en/Our-Work/Dropout-Prevention/~/media/Files/Our percent20Work/
    Cities_In_Crisis_Report_2009.ashx.

14 McKinsey Global Institute, "The Economic Impact of the Achievement Gap in America's Schools:
    Summary of Findings" (April 2009),
    www.mckinsey.com/clientservice/socialsector/achievement_gap_report.pdf.

15 Center for Research on Education Outcomes (CREDO), "Multiple Choice: Charter School Performance
    in 16 States," Stanford University (June 2009), 3,
    www.credo.stanford.edu/reports/MULTIPLE_CHOICE_CREDO.pdf.

Chapter 31

16 Robert J. LaLonde, "The Case for Wage Insurance," Council on Foreign Relations, CSR No. 30
    (September 2007), www.cfr.org/publication/13661/case_for_wage_insurance.html.

17 Carlos Anrisano, et al, "Accounting for the Cost of Health Care in the United States," McKinsey Global
    Institute (January 2007), 13–19.

Chapter 32

18 Jeffrey S. Passel and D'Vera Cohn, "U.S. Population Projects: 2005–2050," Pew Hispanic Center, Pew
    Research Center (February 11, 2008), www.pewhispanic.org/files/reports/85.pdf.

19 Uri Dadush and Bennett Stancil, "The World Order in 2050, Policy Outlook," The Carnegie Endowment
    for International Peace (April 2010), 8, www.carnegieendowment.org/files/World_Order_in_2050.pdf.

Chapter 33

20 U.S. Department of Commerce, "Connection, Performance, Impact, Moving Forward 2009,"
    International Trade Administration (n.d.), 10, www.trade.gov/cs/cs_annualreport09.pdf.

21 Fareed Zakaria, *The Post-American World* (New York: W. W. Norton Company, 2008), 207.

Chapter 35

22 Alan Greenspan, "Fear Undermines America's Recovery," *Financial Times* (October 7, 2010).

Chapter 37

23 Pew Charitable Trust, "Majority Sees U.S. Leadership in Space as Essential: Shuttle Program Viewed as a Good Investment" (July 5, 2011), www.pewresearch.org/pubs/2047/poll-space-exploration-shuttle-program-final-mission.

Chapter 40

24 Diane Farrell, et al, "The Emerging Global Labor Market: Part 1—The Demand for Offshore Talent in Services," McKinsey Global Institute (June 2005), 35.

25 James Lamont, "US Proves Call Centre Match for India Over Hire Costs," Financial Times (August 18, 2010).

Chapter 41

26 David Barboza, "China's Cities Piling Up Debt To Fuel Boom," *The New York Times* (July 7, 2011).

27 Martin Wolf, "How China Could Yet Fail Like Japan," *Financial Times* (June 15, 2011).

28 Kevin Lim, "'Meaningful Probability' of a China Hard Landing: Roubini," *Reuters* (June 13, 2011), www.reuters.com/article/2011/06/13/us-roubini-idUSTRE75C1OF20110613.

29 *The Economist,* "Special Report: China: Rising Power, Anxious State" (June 25, 2011), 5.

ACKNOWLEDGEMENTS

THIS BOOK HAS BEEN a long journey and there are thanks to give.

Like most people who start a hobby outside of their day job, the effort of writing this book fell mainly in the evenings and on the weekends and often took precious time away from my family. I could never have finished this effort without the support of such an amazing family. To my wife, Martina, and my daughters, Kaya and Anka, I give my thanks for their love, support, and above all their complete faith that I could and would actually finish the darn thing. In particular, my thanks to Martina for keeping me on track and being a project manager on everything from book covers to web sites. I could not have done this without her.

Work is next. I wear several hats in addition to writing. One of those is a day job in the IT industry. When I presented this book to my company with my desire to publish, they were exceedingly generous despite the provocative nature of the title and content. They said fine, but with the provision that I did not use the company's name or involve the company in any way. These are, after all, not company positions, but my own personal opinions. I have done all I can to honor their faith in me. There are individuals to thank for offering encouragement along the way. They include Erich, Andy, Tom, and Jeff. My thanks to my colleagues at work including Carole, Leslie, Greg, Damon, Matthew, and Natalie. I truly appreciate their support.

Early on when I got involved with outsourcing, I joined an organization called the International Association of Outsourcing Professionals (IAOP) to begin understanding this industry. My own interest was in the human and political dimensions and key leadership in IAOP has been very supportive of exploring this issue. I would like to give special thanks to Michael Corbett, Debi Hamill, and their staff at IAOP. Another person who offered encouragement early on was Atul Vashistha with Neo Group. And finally, my colleagues on IAOP's sub-committee on Corporate Social

Responsibility and Outsourcing deserve special mention: Ron Babin, Bill Hefley, Pam O'Dell, and a strong group from companies and organizations as diverse as Digital Divide Data, the Rockefeller Foundation, and several firms.

I would be extremely remiss if I didn't mention some old friends. Moving from California to Portland, I've lost touch with some of them, but they listened to the very long and slow evolution of this thesis over the years with great patience and encouragement over campfires and in pubs. They kept me down to earth while still offering encouragement. They are Larry, Rod, Tony, Pavel, Andre, and Tom to name just a few who were regaled the most.

Toby Lester also deserves special mention for providing early encouragement at several points from his perspective both as an experienced editor and now as an extraordinarily talented author in his own right with several books under his belt.

When it came time to move this book into production, it was a team effort. There were a number of people that played critical and important roles and deserve a very special thank you. Kay Tracy for early reviews. Ali McCart for her exceptional editorial work. Olga Bosak of All Elements Design for original design work. Anita Jones for final cover design and the laborious work of interior design – especially after I changed the requirements multiple times. Pamela Ivey stepped in at the end to index the final product and I truly appreciate her help. And finally Laura Templin for an exceptional eye and the ability to turn an imperfect subject into a decent author photo. Thank you all for your incredible help.

Last, a long distance thank you. I believe you are what you read. For a number of years I have been reading the *Financial Times, New York Times, Foreign Affairs,* and *The Atlantic.* My thinking has been shaped by some of the brightest and most talented journalists and writers out there and I want to thank them for the great work that they do every day, without which I could never have completed this book.

Scott Phillips
Portland, Oregon
March, 2012

INDEX

ABOUT THE AUTHOR

Scott Phillips has over 15 years of experience in the Information Technology industry of global consulting and outsourcing services. Prior to his IT career, he was a Peace Corps volunteer and headquarters staff member. These two disparate careers provide a unique perspective for looking at the moral case on outsourcing.

Author photograph by Laura Templin / Laura's Photography

Alitum Press
www.alitumpress.com

Made in the USA
Middletown, DE
06 December 2018